HOW TO PASS

INTERMEDIATE 2
HISTORY

John A. Kerr

Hodder Gibson

A MEMBER OF THE HODDER HEADLINE GROUP

For Ruby Robinson, the future in the past again

The Publishers would like to thank the following for permission to reproduce copyright material:
Photo credits
Page 38 Hulton Archive/Getty Images; Page 40 Dorothea Lange/Library Of Congress/Getty Images; Page 42 Bettmann/Corbis; Page 52 Doug Houghton/Alamy; Page 57 Corbis; Page 61 www.annanphotographs.co.uk; Page 68 Newsquest (Herald & Times). Licensor www.scran.ac.uk; Page 74 Mary Evans/The Women's Library; Page 79 Bettmann/Corbis; Page 84 Bettmann/Corbis; Page 90 Bettmann/Corbis; Page 96 Ullsteinbild/TopFoto
Acknowledgements
Extracts from question papers are reprinted with permission of the Scottish Qualifications Authority.
Every effort has been made to trace all copyright holders, but if any have been inadvertently overlooked the Publishers will be pleased to make the necessary arrangements at the first opportunity.

Although every effort has been made to ensure that website addresses are correct at time of going to press, Hodder Gibson cannot be held responsible for the content of any website mentioned in this book. It is sometimes possible to find a relocated web page by typing in the address of the home page for a website in the URL window of your browser.

Hachette's policy is to use papers that are natural, renewable and recyclable products and made from wood grown in sustainable forests. The logging and manufacturing processes are expected to conform to the environmental regulations of the country of origin.

Orders: please contact Bookpoint Ltd, 130 Milton Park, Abingdon, Oxon OX14 4SB. Telephone: (44) 01235 827720. Fax: (44) 01235 400454. Lines are open 9.00 – 5.00, Monday to Saturday, with a 24-hour message answering service. Visit our website at www.hoddereducation.co.uk. Hodder Gibson can be contacted direct on: Tel: 0141 848 1609; Fax: 0141 889 6315; email: hoddergibson@hodder.co.uk

Cover photo Andrea Pistolesi/The Image Bank/Getty Images
Illustrations by Ian Heard, Redmoor Design
Typeset in 9.5/12.5pt Frutiger Light by Phoenix Photosetting, Chatham, Kent
Printed in Great Britain by Martins The Printers, Berwick-upon-Tweed

A catalogue record for this title is available from the British Library

ISBN-13: 978 0340 946 343

CONTENTS

Contents

INTRODUCTION

If you are studying Intermediate 2 History then this book is for you.

This book was written to provide a useful guide to Intermediate 2 history students who are aiming not just to pass their exam but to pass well.

This book will help you to revise what you need to know in the exam and how to answer the questions.

What is in this book?

It starts by giving some advice on how to learn and revise more effectively and efficiently.

It shows you how to produce the best possible answers to all the different types of questions in the Intermediate 2 exam.

It provides advice about what you need to know for the eight most popular topics studied at Intermediate 2.

It also shows you how to produce your best possible Extended Response.

How to be a better learner

Before you start revising all the information you have to know for the exam, have you thought about how efficiently you learn? Do you spend hours just reading notes over and over again? Revise for a while then ask yourself some serious questions. How much of your revision can you really remember an hour after you have finished? How much can you remember the next day? How much can you remember next week?

The following activities are just some examples of activities that will help you to revise for any subject, not just history.

But why bother doing different things?

Think about this:

If you always do what you have always done....
then you will always get what you have always got.

If you really want to improve then things have to change. They will not change just because you want them to. You have the power to make a difference to yourself.

The pyramid of efficiency

The pyramid diagram (page 2) shows on average what a person will remember 24 hours after a 'learning experience' if they do nothing to reinforce it. For example, if you sit and read over information and then do nothing to reinforce that reading then after 24 hours you will have forgotten 90% of the information you read. That is not the best way to use your time.

On the other hand, if you try to explain clearly what you have recently revised to a friend then you are using your learning for a purpose. That means you can expect to remember over 75% of what you revised. The same is true if you just record your thoughts or information onto disc, tape or video. So it makes sense to think about HOW you intend to learn.

This pyramid shows what percentage of new information an average person would remember (or retain) after 24 hours if they used the methods of learning shown here – AND if that person did nothing to reinforce the learning during the following 24 hours.

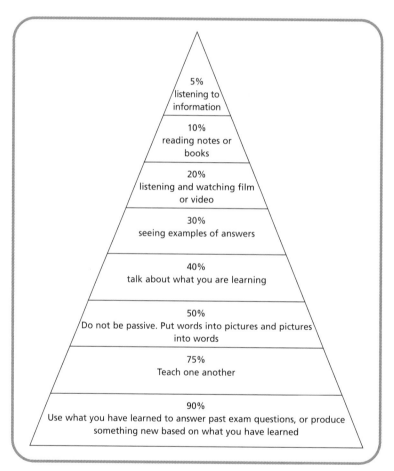

5%
listening to information

10%
reading notes or books

20%
listening and watching film or video

30%
seeing examples of answers

40%
talk about what you are learning

50%
Do not be passive. Put words into pictures and pictures into words

75%
Teach one another

90%
Use what you have learned to answer past exam questions, or produce something new based on what you have learned

A pyramid divided into 'best learning' methods

The 'I really know this!' test

Think of a place you know really well. It could be a room in your house, a shop or a street or a quiet place you like.

From your memory, describe, list or draw in detail all the things you can see in your place. Try to be as detailed as you can, such as colours and patterns and where all the things are in relation to each other.

Next time you go to that place take your list with you. When you get there you will recognise instantly every single detail but do those details appear on your list? I bet they don't.

The point is that recognising lots of detail is not the same as knowing it.

Now think about your revision. If you read over the same book or notes again and again you will feel you know it but you are really just recognising your notes. Without the prompt of your notes in front of you, can you really be sure you know the information well enough to use it in an exam?

In the next few pages, you will find tips and ideas for making your revision more effective and maybe even more enjoyable.

How do you know what to revise?

Your brain works best when it has a definite purpose to perform or a puzzle to solve so try this.

List maker

Key Points

- ◆ Step 1: Decide on a focused topic or question from the unit you have been studying.

- ◆ Step 2: BEFORE you do ANY revision on this topic, write a list of all that you already know about the subject. It might be quite a long list but you only need to write it once. It shows you all the information that is in your long-term memory so you now know what you do not have to revise – you already know it! And now you know what you do have to revise!

- ◆ Step 3: Now do your revision – and this time you have a purpose. You are now looking for new information. When you have finished this session of revision, write a new list of the new information you have learned.

- ◆ Step 4: Now colour-shade each list a different colour. That will make each list easier to see in your mind's eye.

- ◆ Step 5: A day after your revision, try to remember as much as you can from the new learning box. That is what you need to reinforce so remember the colour of the new learning box and think what you wrote in it.

- ◆ Step 6: Check back to remind yourself what you wrote in the new learning box and then try to remember it all sometime later. Each time you do that you reinforce your new learning.

Here's another idea to help your learning. It's called Stop and Review.

Key Points

◆ Step 1: When you have done no more than 5 minutes of revision STOP!

◆ Step 2: Write a heading in your own words which sums up the topic you have been revising.

◆ Step 3: Write a summary in no more than two sentences of what you have revised. Don't fool yourself. If you cannot do it or do not want to do it why not? Don't ever say to yourself, 'I know it but I cannot put it into words'. That just means you don't know it well enough. So if you cannot write your summary, then revise that section again, knowing that you must write a summary at the end of it. I guarantee your revision will suddenly improve. Your brain now knows exactly what it has to do. You will learn much more effectively.

Use technology!

Why should everything be written down? Have you thought about ideas maps, diagrams, cartoons and colour to help you learn?

Rather than write down notes why not record your revision material onto an MP3 player, mini disc or tapes? Why not make a video diary where you tell the camera what you are doing, what you think you have learned and what you still have to do? You could share these things with your friends. They deserve a laugh. Nobody said revision had to be boring. And after you gain the results you want, you can watch the videos again and wonder why you got so stressed in the first place!

Word search work out

You need to work with a partner on the word search activity.

Choose a topic to revise.

Design a word search about 10 squares by 10 squares. It's your choice but keep it realistic.

Your puzzle must only contain facts linked to the topic you are revising. You can do others which, for example, focus on ideas, names or vocabulary.

The words/phrases can go in any direction and phrases can be split.

Do not indicate the words in your puzzle by highlighting them.

Each word/phrase must have a definition or clue to help someone find the words/phrases. Write these definitions beside or below your word search.

When you have completed your puzzle, exchange it with your partner and use the definitions to the puzzle you received to find the answers.

Why do this?

◆ By doing the word search you must know or find out detailed information.

◆ You must know how to spell your information.

◆ You must know what the information means exactly before you can write your definition.

◆ You must know more information to solve your partner's word search.

◆ All the time your brain is active, not passive hoping to 'memorise'.

Pictures or words

There is a lot of advice given here in words. But the ideas map on page 6 shows many different ideas on how to make your revision more effective and enjoyable.

To make yourself really think about the ideas on the map draw it yourself.

Add colour, perhaps colour-coding revision methods that you have tried, will try, may try and those you really do not want to do.

Then add as many new ideas about how to revise as you can. Once again you are forcing your brain to be active.

Try to add as many new ideas to the map as possible.

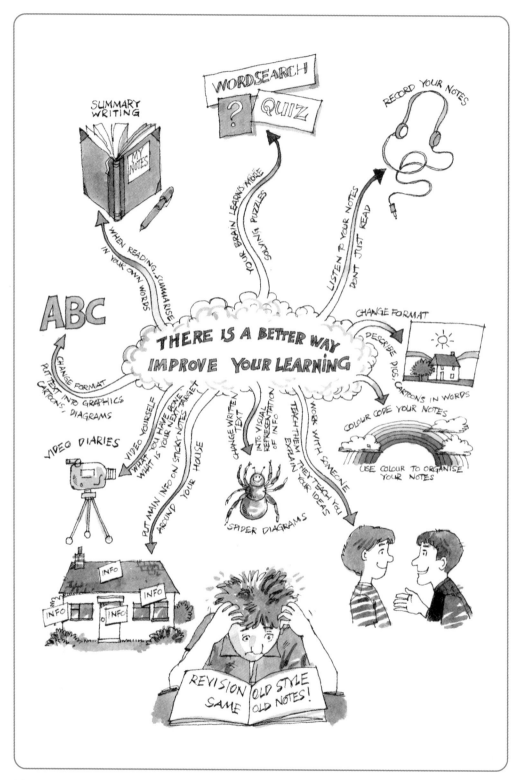

Ideas map

SECTION 1

JARGON BUSTER

During your Intermediate 2 History course you will read certain words and phrases that are relevant to the content of your course, the assessments or the final exam. You will also read these words and phrases elsewhere in this book.

This section explains the meanings of most of those words and phrases.

Key Words and Definitions

- **Compare:** Look for the differences and similarities between two sources. Do not just describe each source. You must link connected points from each source and show how they agree or disagree with each other.
- **Context:** What was happening at the time the source was produced.
- **Describe:** A describe question asks you to tell what happened. You do NOT need to give reasons why things happened. In a describe question, just tell the story that is relevant to the question giving the facts in the right order.
- **Explain:** An explain question asks for reasons why something happened. It is never enough just to tell a story in an explain question.
- **Extended response:** This is an essay, done in class but marked by Scottish Qualification Authority (SQA) markers. You have 1 hour to write this essay but you will be well prepared and allowed to refer to a 150 word plan you have written out already. There is more on the extended response later in this book.
- **Historical study: Scottish and British contexts:** This is part 2 of your exam paper. You must choose at least ONE of the contexts and no more than two of them. Examples of contexts in this section are: 'Wallace, Bruce and the Wars of Independence 1286–1328' and 'From the Cradle to the Grave? Social Welfare in Britain 1890s–1951'.
- **Historical study: European and World contexts:** This is part 3 of your exam paper. You must choose at least ONE of the contexts and no more than two of them. Examples of contexts in this section are: 'Race Relations in the USA 1918–1968' and the 'Road to War 1933–1939'.
- **NABS:** (sometimes referred to as Unit Assessments). NABS are provided by the SQA and they are pass or fail assessments. If some parts of your NAB assessment are not very good, your teacher/tutor might ask you to 'revisit' those parts but more usually you will be allowed to sit another NAB on that topic later in the course. You must achieve a pass in one NAB for each context studied, as well as your final exam, to be awarded a full Intermediate 2 certificate.
- **Origin:** This means where a source comes from or who produced it.
- **Produced:** This means how a source was created, for example a speech, something written or something drawn or photographed. You must also place the source in its CONTEXT.
- **Purpose:** This is why the source was produced.

Key Words and Definitions continued ➤

Key Words *and* **Definitions** *continued*

◆ **Recall or recalled knowledge:** This is your own knowledge about a topic, either used to develop information given to you in sources or as stand-alone information not prompted by the sources.

◆ **Reliable:** This means how much you can trust a source to tell the truth. Consider if the source is one sided (biased), propaganda, exaggeration or deliberate lies. It's best to quote evidence from the source to back up your claim if you think it is biased.

◆ **Short essay:** The Short Essay is the first part of your exam paper and it is worth 8 marks.

There is one essay title for each of the contexts you have studied. Your must choose ONE title to answer.

Your answer must be in the style of an essay.

You should use between 15 and 20 minutes of your exam time for the essay.

◆ **SQA:** The Scottish Qualifications Authority is the organisation that decides what you have to know and what you must be able to do before you can be given an Intermediate 2 award in History. It provides the assessments (the NABS) and also sets the exam and marks your answers. Finally, the SQA issues you with your Intermediate 2 certificate.

◆ **Useful:** You will be asked 'how useful' a certain source is as evidence. That means you must give reasons why it would be useful for finding out about something and also why its use might be limited. Then reach a conclusion by deciding just how useful it is.

◆ **Valuable:** This is similar to a 'how useful' question. The value of a source is its usefulness as evidence for finding out as much as possible about a certain event.

Learning Outcomes

There are three Learning Outcomes assessed throughout your course. They are known as LO1, LO2 and LO3. Sometimes you will see LO1, 2 or 3 written at the side of your class work or National Assessment Bank (NABS) answers. That's because your teacher is not just marking what you know about a subject but also your skills in using the information you have.

◆ **LO1 Learning outcome 1:** LO1 questions are usually questions that ask you to describe something. To achieve LO1, you must show off what you know about the contexts you have studied.

◆ **LO2 Learning outcome 2:** To achieve LO2, you must be able to give reasons to explain why things happened. In LO2 answers, the information you use must be relevant and accurate. Sometimes you will be able to select information from sources in the exam paper to help you. You must also have a conclusion which sums up your overall answer to the question.

◆ **LO3 Learning outcome 3:** LO3 questions are evaluation questions. They usually have 'how useful', 'how reliable' or 'how valuable' in them.

To achieve LO3, you must be able to evaluate historical sources and also place these sources in context. You will be told where a source comes from so it's up to you to use that information to help explain, for example, why the source might be useful or reliable. You should also mention why the source was written. That will help you to judge how useful or reliable or how biased a source might be. You should also be able to mention in your answer how detailed and accurate the information in the source is by matching it up with your own knowledge.

The main thing in LO3 questions is to judge the source, not describe it.

THE EXTENDED RESPONSE

Now you have some ideas about how to revise, it is time to move on to thinking about how to get the best marks possible for the exam.

Put simply, there are TWO parts to the Intermediate 2 examination.

The FIRST part of your exam is the Extended Response. Most people write their Extended Response in the Spring term, a few weeks before the exam in May.

The SECOND part is the exam you will sit in May. Much more on that later!

What is the Extended Response?

The Extended Response is an essay written under exam conditions and then sent to the SQA to be marked.

Why do I have to do an Extended Response?

It's a chance to show off what you can do! In the final exam, you have very limited time and markers know that answers written under exam pressure are not likely to show the best you can do. The Extended Response gives you the chance to write the best essay you can.

Why is the Extended Response very important?

It is really important to do as well as you can in the Extended Response as the mark you get is part of your final Intermediate 2 exam award total. In fact, the Extended Response counts for 20 marks out of a total of 70 so doing well in the Extended Response can provide you with a very useful launch pad for future success.

How long does my essay have to be?

The answer is simple – what you can write in 1 hour! There are NO word limits in the Extended Response. Most people can write one page of A4 in 10 minutes. As there are 6×10 minutes in 1 hour then it is possible to write a six-page essay and some people do. The bulk of essays are about 4 or 5 pages long.

Should I try to choose a title that is fresh and new and different?

You don't have to. Some candidates make life difficult for themselves by making up difficult titles for their essay. Ask your teacher or tutor if you are unsure. It's not necessary to invent a completely new title. Perfectly good essays can be written from titles taken from past Intermediate 2 exam papers.

Are there types of questions to avoid?

Yes. First of all your question must be part of the syllabus you are studying. So an essay about events in the Second World War or about the Causes of the First World War would risk gaining 0 marks as it is not within any Intermediate 2 syllabus. Your essay titles MUST be part of the Intermediate 2 History syllabus, checkable at: www.sqa.org.uk.

Second, your essay title should be based on a question that allows you to use your evidence to answer the question. Titles such as 'Why did the Liberals tackle the problem of poverty in the early twentieth century?' are good.

On the other hand, try to avoid titles that are just statements. Essays with headings such as 'The Slave Trade' or 'The Crusades' or 'Appeasement' are very likely to fail because the marker has no way of knowing what you are trying to do apart from write a description of the subject in the title. A good way to make sure your essay is issue based is to include words such as 'To what extent' or 'Explain why', for example, 'Explain why women had not achieved the vote by 1914'.

Finally, try NOT to make up questions that are too complicated or that ask two questions within the same title. A useful tip is to see if you have used the word 'and' in the title. If you have then you might have made up two questions. An example of a double question is, 'Why did the Liberal Reforms happen and how successful were they?' That's bad enough but think of the work involved in writing this essay done by a person some years ago – 'Why did the Act of Union take place, who was against it and why and who was for it and why?'

Remember you are in charge of choosing your questions so why make life difficult for yourself?

What if my Extended Response title appears in the final exam?

You just got lucky!

If you choose your Extended Response from 'mainstream titles' it is quite possible your topic, and perhaps even a title similar to your Extended Response, will appear in the final exam. There is NO restriction about answering that question using the memory you have of doing the Extended Response. But be careful to adapt your information to fit the exact question asked in the exam.

What is the Extended Response plan?

Your plan provides a framework and notes for your essay. It shows a marker that you have researched, selected and organised your information. It shows you have thought about your work and reached a decision about the question in your title. Your Extended Response plan MUST be sent to the SQA with your finished essay, preferably on the official form downloadable from the SQA website at www.sqa.org.uk. The main point of doing that is to include a word count in the box provided. You must use no more than 150 words. However, your plan can be spread over as many pages as you like if it helps you. Just attach it to the official form.

Is the plan really a plan?

It depends on you. Most people have written their Extended Response several times before they write the final copy under exam conditions. By doing that you have several advantages.

First of all you allow yourself a chance to rethink and edit your work.

It is your choice if you word process or hand write at this stage. Word processed work is easier to change by cutting and pasting, spell checking and so on. But handwriting is practice for the time you will have in the exam and also, by rewriting over again, you will establish your essay in your memory.

Once your draft has been written, you may be lucky enough to have a teacher or tutor who will read over your essay and make suggestions.

Finally, when you have rewritten the essay two or three times you will have a fairly clear idea of what you will write and how long it will take you. Now you must break the essay down into a helpful plan of 150 words.

How should I write and use my plan?

Your plan should be exactly that – a plan of the essay you will write. Your plan should NOT be just a collection of facts, figures and quotes. It is a PLAN! It should outline the main parts of your essay and remind you what to write.

my title

my plan

   introduction

      main paragraph 1

      main paragraph 2

      main paragraph 3

      main paragraph 4

      main paragraph 5

      main paragraph 6

   conclusion

   useful quotes

Will my plan be marked?

The plan is NOT marked but is a vital part of your essay both for your use and for markers to see that you have completed the required planning stage. Nor is there any time limit to a plan. The plan is YOURS. You can change it, colour it or print it out. You can write it anywhere, anytime before you write your Extended Response under exam conditions.

Are there any rules about the plan?

Yes, there is one absolute rule. Your plan must NOT be longer than 150 words. You WILL have marks deducted from your final essay mark if you go over that limit.

Are diagrams and pictures allowed in the plan?

No. The SQA are aware of some people trying to get round the rules by using code words or pictograms. The SQA's position on this is clear: 'Plans may be in the form of a diagram but plain English must be used – not text or pictures. For example, drawings of the layout of Stirling Bridge or Bannockburn are not allowed.'

Can I use abbreviations?

Yes, but what's the point? Each abbreviation will still be counted as a word so abbreviations will not reduce your total number of words!

How should I begin my plan?

It is sometimes hard to start writing if you have not thought through your answer so be prepared and use your introduction to your advantage. You could use about 40–50 words to outline your introduction quite fully. That would get you started and give you a chance to outline the main parts of the essay that you will develop later. As you write the later parts of your essay, you could refer back to your introduction as a guide to help you remember what to write about next.

How should I plan the middle part of my Extended Response?

You should aim to write a main starting sentence to begin each paragraph.

If you are intending to write 5 or 6 paragraphs, each one in your plan should be allocated 10 words. That means you will use about 50 or 60 words.

Remember you should use supporting evidence throughout your essay. History skills should run through the essay, so that means you must not only use factual detail but also be prepared to use quotes and make reference if you can to the reliability and accuracy of the information used.

If you are using quotes, do not waste words copying them out fully in your plan. Each quote should be boiled down to essential words to prompt your memory.

It is also helpful to remind yourself to include mini conclusions linking each paragraph back to the main title, so you keep your arguments going and don't fall back into story telling with little connection to the main question.

How should I organise my conclusion?

You must have a strong conclusion. A report from the SQA said that, 'In poorer essays the conclusion was little more than a repetition of the introduction and did not use the evidence in the development'. So you should really work on your conclusion.

It is really important to summarise your main ideas and explain what you think the most important point in your answer is. If you have followed the word allocation so far you will have about 50 words for this. That's about six lines of normal writing! So you could really work on your conclusion and have most of it in your plan. And remember – try to ensure your conclusion ends on a high note, perhaps with an appropriate quote that provides an overall answer to the question that supports your main argument.

Is there anything else I can do to prepare effectively?

The layout of your plan can be made to work for you. Empty space is free and so are arrows, lines and boxes so use them all to help you to lay out your plan so you can see what is going where and in what order.

What does a weak plan look like?

The first plan is based around the title 'Why did Robert the Bruce succeed in gaining Scottish independence while others had failed?'.

> ## Example
>
> Here is a weak plan
>
> Alexander 111 died. Margaret, maid of Norway Orkneys died
>
> Edward 1
>
> Competitors John Balliol. Overlord.
>
> Wallace Stirling Bridge Falkirk, captured, London, executed as lesson to others.
>
> Bruce Comyn Dumfries Kirk murder, excommunicated
>
> Outlaw. Barbour's Bruce.
>
> Spider
>
> Declaration of Clergy
>
> guerrilla war (secret war)
>
> recapture castles
>
> Stirling
>
> Midsummer Day
>
> Earl of Somerset
>
> Bannockburn
>
> river marshy
>
> little folk
>
> victory
>
> not end of war
>
> Treaty of Northampton, treaty of Edinburgh
>
> Scotland free.

Why is this a weak plan?

The main problem with this plan is it does not help to answer the question set. There are no ideas outlined and no real indication how the 'why others failed' part of the question will be answered. But there are other weaknesses.

First of all it only uses about half the available words. The plan itself is not even a plan. It is really just a long list of information and it looks as if the candidate will have to do all his or her thinking during the exam write-up time.

Some of the information is also irrelevant to the question. Why waste words on 'spider' and 'little folk' when they have little or nothing to do with the question asked?

Example

This next plan is much better.

Introduction

Many reasons succeeded. Military/ diplomatic

Others – Balliol, Wallace/Moray failed. Why?

Unsuccessful Death Alexander/Margaret; Great Cause; Edward chose Balliol – failed retain independence – vassal, war, Dunbar, humiliation.

Wallace/Moray 1296 – resistance, Stirling Bridge, Guardian Scotland but trusted? Moray died.

1297 defeat Falkirk. Loses support. Wallace captured executed. Leaderless

Bruce – legitimate challenger. Comyn murder turning point.

Bruce unlikely leader. Perth defeat. Church excommunication?

How recover?

Military

Defeat Comyn's allies – establishing authority; 'Secret war' – guerrilla attacks on English. Bannockburn – importance – Scotland united. English beatable. All castles Scots hands.

Raids in England – raise money, weaken England

Diplomatic

Declaration Clergy – Church on side

Declaration Nobility – nobles ditto

Loyalty – 'Disinherited'; defeat rebellion. Declaration of Arbroath – importance – people's choice – Bruce legitimate – Pope approval

Northampton/Edinburgh - independent Scotland.

Example continued ➤

Example *continued*

Other reasons

Edward 1 long dead, Edward 11 not aggressive.

English political difficulties distract attention.

Stability – succession, legislation, administration.

Conclusion

Authority, effective war leader

diplomatic/military tactics, luck.

Why is this a better plan?

Mainly because it allows the person writing it to use the plan as a step-by-step guide. The word allowance of 150 is almost fully used and there are few, if any, wasted words such as 'and' or 'is'.

It also shows the structure of the essay. By leaving lines between sections the writer can see where new paragraphs start.

The introduction and conclusion are clearly marked to remind the writer they must be included.

Earlier you read about using 50 words for your introduction, 50 for your development and 50 for your conclusion. This plan shows another way of writing a plan.

The main point is to write a plan that helps you – and that means the hard thinking part of the essay happens before and during the plan writing – not later!

Summary

- Your plan should use all the words allowed in the plan.
- The plan should be a guide to how the essay will look.
- It must help to answer the question asked, not just be a list of unconnected facts.

Now you are ready to write your Extended Response.

For more advice about writing all essays, whether they are 'short essays' in the exam, essays for internal assessment or your Extended Response, turn to Chapter 4 giving advice about short essay writing.

THE EXAM PAPER

 ## What do I have to do in the exam?

Before the exam, make sure you have seen what a real Intermediate 2 paper looks like. It is coloured light green and the instructions about what to answer are usually on page 2. The context names are listed on page 3.

Instructions

Answer **one** question from Part 1, The Short Essay.

Answer **one** context from Part 2, Scottish and British.

Answer **one** context from Part 3, European and World.

Answer **one** other context from

either Part 2, Scottish and British

or Part 3, European and World

Contents

Part 1   Short Essay Questions
      Answer one question only

Part 2   Scottish and British Contexts

1. Murder in the Cathedral: Crown, Church and People, 1154–1173.
2. Wallace, Bruce and the Wars of Independence, 1286–1328.
3. Mary Queen of Scots and the Scottish Reformation, 1540s–1587.
4. The Coming of the Civil War, 1603–1642.
5. "Ane End of Ane Auld Sang": Scotland and the Treaty of Union, 1690s–1715.
6. Immigrants and Exiles: Scotland, 1830s–1930s.
7. (a)   From the Cradle to the Grave? Social Welfare in Britain, 1890s–1951.
      OR
   (b)   Campaigning for Change: Social Change in Scotland, 1900s–1979.
8. A Time of Troubles: Ireland, 1900–1923.

Part 3   European and World Contexts

1. The Norman Conquest, 1060–1153.
2. The Cross and the Crescent: The First Crusade, 1096–1125.
3. War, Death and Revolt in Medieval Europe, 1328–1436.
4. New Worlds: Europe in the Age of Expansion, 1480s–1530s.
5. Tea and Freedom: The American Revolution, 1763–1783.
6. "This Accursed Trade": The British Slave Trade and its Abolition, 1770–1807.
7. Citizens! The French Revolution, 1789–1794.
8. Cavour, Garibaldi and the Making of Italy, 1815–1870.
9. Iron and Blood? Bismarck and the Creation of the German Empire, 1815–1871.
10. The Red Flag: Lenin and the Russian Revolution, 1894–1921.
11. Free at Last? Race Relations in the USA, 1918–1968.
12. The Road to War, 1933–1939.
13. In the Shadow of the Bomb: The Cold War, 1945–1985.

Key Points

- You MUST choose one title from part 1 and write a short essay that answers your chosen title.
- You MUST choose one context from part 2 which is about Scottish/British subjects.
- You MUST choose one context from part 3 which is about European/World subjects. There will also be three sources that can be used in some of the questions.
- You MUST do one other set of questions from one other context. You have a free choice here – the context you choose can be from either Scottish/British subjects or European/World subjects.

Turn to the correct page for your first context and get started.

It's vital to use time effectively.

You have 1 hour 45 minutes (105 minutes) to do A SHORT ESSAY PLUS 9 QUESTIONS.

In total, your exam paper is worth 50 marks. When you divide the number of marks into the time available you will see that works out at about 2 minutes per mark. That leaves you 5 minutes surplus to use at the beginning of the exam to settle and make your choices.

Hints and Tips

It is usually best to leave the short essay until last. That way you know how much time you have for it and you can plan it out more carefully.

Here is one way of creating time for a good short essay.

Each context should take you NO MORE than 28 minutes. Aim for 25 minutes. That means you should use about 8 minutes for each separate question.

Once you have answered three contexts you should have used no more than 75 minutes. That means you have about 30 minutes left to write a really good short essay. You can now take a few minutes to make your choice of title, plan your essay and show off what you know.

ANSWERING SHORT ESSAY QUESTIONS

How do I do the short essay?

Part 1 of your exam booklet is called the 'The Short Essay'. Your list of choices usually starts on page 4 of the exam booklet.

You will see there is one essay title for each of the contexts you have studied.

You must choose ONE title to answer.

Your short essay is like any other essay: it must be structured with a beginning, middle and an end.

Your answer must be relevant to the question.

The first part of your essay should be an introduction which sets the context of the question and outlines the main ideas you will develop.

The second part should show off your knowledge in several paragraphs.

The final part should be a conclusion which answers the question asked.

What will the essay questions be like?

ALL short essays have a similar style of question. You will never get a 'tell a story' essay which asks you only to 'describe'. You will often be asked to write an essay about why something happened.

Example

Explain why the reforms of the Labour Government after 1945 can be described as setting up a 'Welfare State'.

Explain why Robert the Bruce won the battle of Bannockburn in 1314.

Explain the importance of Martin Luther King to the Civil Rights Movement in the USA.

Questions can also ask you to judge or evaluate events such as 'How successful were the Liberal Reforms of 1906–1914 in meeting the needs of the people?'

Is there a 'must remember' rule about writing essays?

Yes. Answer the question that is asked, not the question you would like to see in the exam paper. Every year markers find some essays that do not directly answer the questions asked in the exam paper. The reason for this is that candidates probably prepared for different questions and were unable to change their answers to fit the new question.

What should I do when I first look at the short essay questions in the exam?

You will be nervous. You will want to get started quickly.

The first thing to do is breathe deeply. Then look for questions you might want to answer. Then make sure you have understood not only what the question is about but also what you have to do. In other words, see what the topic is but also what the task is that you have to do.

Finally, read all the questions again and make sure the one you have chosen gives you the best chance to score highly.

Is it enough just to write out as much information as I know?

No, it is not. Essay writing is about knowing detailed information BUT it is even more important to know the process and technique of HOW to write a good essay.

 Why is an introduction important?

Your introduction should provide you with a guide to follow through the rest of the essay.

The introduction is where you must do your hardest thinking about the topic and the task and what will be the main stages of your answer.

Without an introduction there will be no structure because you have not thought HOW you intend to answer the question.

If you have not got a rough plan in your head, your essay risks becoming just a story and may not gain many marks.

What is the difference between a poor introduction and a good one?

To answer that question it is best to use some real examples.

Suppose the first question you look at is this: 'Explain why the reforms of the Labour Government after 1945 can be described as setting up a "Welfare State".'

Example

This is a very weak introduction

'In order to answer this question it is necessary to explain why the reforms of the Labour Government after 1945 can be described as setting up a "Welfare State". The Labour Government started the National Health Service and built more houses for people.'

 Why is this a very weak introduction?

Time is wasted by almost writing out the whole question. All it does is pretend to be an introduction.

There is no thought here about what the main stages of the essay will be about or how the essay will develop.

There is no sign-posting of any ideas about why Labour's reforms can be described as setting up a Welfare State.

The second sentence is just a mention of two of the changes made by the Labour Government without linking them to the main question.

Example

Here is a much better introduction

'A Welfare State means the government looks after the well being or welfare of its people. Between 1945 and 1951 the Labour Government tackled the five giant problems facing Britain. These problems were disease, ignorance, idleness, squalor and want. By trying to defeat the giant problems the new Labour Government aimed to improve the lives of British people "from the cradle to the grave".'

Why is this a better introduction?

The five giant problems mentioned provide a structure which the candidate can follow through the rest of the exam.

It makes clear what a welfare state is. It uses the 'five giants' as a guide. In the rest of the essay, the writer will explain how Labour's reforms tried to solve each of the giant problems.

The writer is familiar with the phrase 'cradle to grave' and that might provide a way of directly answering the question in the conclusion.

There is no irrelevance and it is clear to a marker that the writer understands the question.

Developing the essay

Any essay must have a beginning, a middle and an end. The middle part of the essay will become the longest part of the essay. It is here that you must develop or write about the points made in your introduction.

Try to have at least five main points in this section. Each point should be developed fully as a paragraph. So your middle section should have at least five paragraphs in it.

Do I have to write a development paragraph for every main point I put in my introduction – and how do I do it?

Yes, you should. In the Labour and the welfare state essay title used already you can see that the introduction referred to the five problems of disease, ignorance, idleness, squalor and want.

Each of your development paragraphs should deal with one of these problems.

What is a good and bad development paragraph?

Here are examples of different development paragraphs from an answer about the welfare state question mentioned earlier. The full title was: 'Explain why the reforms of the Labour Government after 1945 can be described as setting up a "Welfare State".'

Example

This example of a weak development paragraph is about reforms to improve the nation's health:

'One of the reforms was the health service. Everyone was given help. Now people could go to hospital or visit a doctor. People became much healthier.'

Why is this a weak paragraph?

It is very short. It does have a starting sentence but there is almost no information about the reform.

The paragraph does not try to show how the health service is connected to a welfare state.

This answer suggests that people could not go to doctors or hospitals before the reform. That is not true.

Example

Here is a much better development paragraph:

'One of the problems tackled by Labour's reforms was disease. Disease was tackled by the new National Health Service that started in 1948. The Health Service was free and aimed to provide all the help people could need. The NHS was paid for by taxation raised by the government and by money paid by workers called National Insurance.

The NHS is an example of the government trying to look after the welfare and health of the British people.'

Why is this a much better paragraph?

Because it is almost the opposite of the weak one!

A strong main sentence links to the introduction and lets a marker know what to expect.

There is accurate factual information that is relevant to the question.

There is no doubt this information is being used to make a point.

There is a mini conclusion that links your information back to the main question and makes it quite clear why the factual information is being included in the essay.

Here is another short essay example: 'Explain why so many Irish immigrants arrived in Scotland after 1830'.

Example

Here is a good introduction to the question:

'There were many reasons why so many Irish immigrants arrived in Scotland after 1830.

Many moved to find jobs (1). Others wanted to escape from poverty (2). Scotland was only a short journey away from Ireland (3). In the 1840s a potato famine caused starvation in Ireland so many emigrated to escape death (4).

Letters sent back home from Irish emigrants in Scotland encouraged others to move (5).'

The numbers marked in this introduction show each of the separate points that can be developed later.

Now see the sort of information you would be expected to include in each paragraph to develop it suitably:

1   Scotland was having an industrial revolution in the mid-nineteenth century. New factories needed workers and jobs were easy to get building canals and railways so many Irish moved to Scotland to find work.

2   Many Irish, especially Catholics, worked on farms and faced terrible poverty. The Irish workers got wages and housing. Although conditions in Scotland's cities and factories were bad and wages low they were still an improvement on life in Ireland.

3   Emigrant ships left Ireland for ports such as Liverpool and Glasgow. The fares were cheap and the voyage short.

4   Most of the poor in Ireland depended on potatoes for food. In 1846 a disease called potato blight rotted the harvest. As a result many Irish chose to emigrate rather than starve.

5   Some Irish immigrants in Scotland met prejudice from Scots but the Catholic Church looked after new immigrants. Many Irish did well and settled in Scotland. News of their better life made other Irish want to migrate to Scotland.

Summary

There are certain things that must be in this middle section:

1   Aim to write at least five separate well-developed paragraphs.

2   You must develop one main point per paragraph.

3   Use as much relevant and accurate information as you can.

Ending your essay

Must I finish with a conclusion?

Yes. There are marks given for a conclusion. You cannot gain full marks without a conclusion.

What is a suitable conclusion?

A suitable conclusion is a paragraph at the end of your essay that makes clear you are summing up your essay and providing a final overall answer to the question set. It should be about two sentences long and preferably start with words such as 'Finally…' or 'In conclusion…'.

Are there rules about what should be in a conclusion?

You must make your mind up and answer the main question.

You should also sum up the main points made in your introduction.

To make your conclusion effective and different try to prioritise your reasons. This means you decide which of the many relevant points you raised in your introduction is the most important in the answer to the main question.

NEVER ever add new factual information into your conclusion. A conclusion ends your essay. It should not continue your essay or push it in a new direction by including new information.

Here are examples of good and bad conclusions to the question 'Explain why the reforms of the Labour Government after 1945 can be described as setting up a "Welfare State".'

Example

This is a weak conclusion:

'Labour's reforms set up a welfare state. They helped improve health and housing and education. They also made people less poor but did not solve all the problems in Britain.'

Why is this a weak conclusion?

It is weak because it does not make clear it is a conclusion. Nor does it answer the original question. It simply states that Labour did set up a welfare state but does not sum up the reasons why the reforms can be described as setting up a 'Welfare State'.

Example

Here is a better conclusion:

'In conclusion, between 1945 and 1951 the Labour Government tried to solve the five giant problems that had faced Britain in 1945. Each of the reforms meant that the government took responsibility for looking after the people of Britain from the cradle to the grave. By 1951 the problems of disease, ignorance, poverty, bad housing and unemployment were less serious than they had been in 1945.'

! **Why is this a better conclusion?**

It starts by making clear this is the conclusion. It sums up the problems dealt with by the Labour Government, suggests that improvements had been made and shows clearly that the writer understands what is meant by 'welfare state'.

ANSWERING LEARNING OUTCOME QUESTIONS

Your exam questions will ask different types of questions.

1 You will be asked to describe something. That is a Learning Outcome 1 question.

2 You will be asked to explain something. That is a Learning Outcome 2 question.

3 You will be asked to evaluate sources. That is a Learning Outcome 3 question.

LO1 questions

LO1 questions usually have the word 'describe' in them. To be successful in this question, you must write the story of what happened and aim to include at least FIVE pieces of detailed accurate recall.

In LO1 questions, there is no source to help you with information so your answer will be based on your own recall.

Your information must be relevant and accurate with as much detail as you can manage in 10 minutes.

And remember – answer the question that you are asked, NOT what you would like it to ask.

Use the grid shown here as a self-check guide to answering LO1 questions. When you know you have met each criterion on the list you can be confident you have a good answer.

Your LO1 answer contains	yes	no
a brief introduction which sets the scene or context. at least five different pieces of recalled information. relevant information. detailed information. accurate information. a direct answer to the question.		
If you have ticked yes to everything then your answer is good. If you have ticked a 'no' make sure that that part of your answer is improved.		

Example

Here is an LO1 question example from Context 2, 'Wallace, Bruce and the Wars of Independence, 1286–1328'.

Question: Describe the events that led to the defeat and capture of King John Balliol. (5 marks)

Here is an example of a weak answer:

'Edward chose King John because Edward thought he could control him. King John had been chosen after Margaret of Norway died and Scotland had no King. Edward of England wanted to control Scotland. When King John attacked England, Edward took his revenge by attacking Scotland and capturing King John.'

Why is this a weak answer?

It is very short and does not contain much recalled information.

It contains irrelevant information. The death of Margaret and the choice of Balliol as king have very little to do with the question.

There is very little accurate or detailed information. The question contains the information that King John was defeated and captured. The only relevant recall in the answer is that Edward attacked Scotland.

Example

Here is another answer:

'When King Edward chose John Balliol to be King of Scotland he believed he could control John Balliol. However when King John decided to fight against Edward, the King of England took his revenge.

When Edward of England went to war against France the Scots made an alliance with France against England. Edward was angry. The Scots also attacked the north of England. When Edward invaded Scotland he first of all destroyed the town of Berwick. The Scottish army was defeated at the battle of Dunbar. After that every important town and castle in Scotland surrendered to Edward without a fight. Edward continued to chase King John Balliol and on 2 July 1296 King John surrendered. King John was publicly humiliated by having the symbols of kingship stripped from his clothes. King John was then taken away as a prisoner to London.'

Why is this a better answer?

Use your LO1 marking grid to find out. Each criterion has been met and this answer would get at least four and probably five marks out of five.

Example

Here is an example of an LO1 question from 'Iron and Blood? Bismarck and the Creation of the German Empire, 1815–1871'.

Question: Describe the activities of the German Nationalists between 1815 and 1848. (5 marks)

Here is a good answer to the question:

'The German Nationalists tried to make the people of Germany feel more German. The Nationalists wanted Germans to share the same national identity.

The Nationalists helped push the French invaders out of their country in 1815.

Writers such as the Brothers Grimm encouraged Germans to realise they shared a common history and language.

Nationalists were proud of the German composer and musician Beethoven. They said Germans had a culture to be proud of.

Many Nationalists wanted to get rid of Austrian power in Germany. At the Hambach festival in 1818 the Nationalist students burned a dummy representing the Austrian Chancellor Metternich. The Nationalists wanted to show they were angry with Austria.

The Nationalists also promoted a song called the Watch of the Rhine as a patriotic song against the French. In 1848 the Nationalists also supported the 1848 revolutions and set up the Frankfurt Parliament in the hope it would help create a united Germany.'

Use the LO1 grid and you will see that:

1 The answer shows the writer knows what the question means.
2 The answer describes the activities of the Nationalists between 1815 and 1848 with reference to both the earlier and later dates within the answer.
3 The answer contains many more than five important pieces of recall.
4 The information contained is detailed and relevant.
5 This answer would get full marks.

Now try some LO1 questions for yourself. You will find some in Section 2.

LO2 questions

To be successful in LO2 answers you must give reasons why something happened or what the consequences or results of something were.

LO2 questions usually start with the words 'Explain why…' or just 'Why…' as in 'Explain why Chamberlain decided to follow a policy of appeasement' or 'Why was the Montgomery Bus Boycott important?'.

In LO2 questions there is a source to help you. In your answer, you must select relevant information from the source and also use accurate and detailed information from your own knowledge.

It would be helpful to start with a brief introduction outlining your main ideas at the start.

The introduction will force you to think what you intend to write. Otherwise you might just start writing a story which is NOT an explanation.

You should end with a short conclusion that sums up your answer to the question.

You should also aim to write your answer in NO MORE THAN 10 minutes.

The grid here is a self-check guide to answering LO2 questions. As the grid reminds you, when you check off every point on the list you can be confident you have a good answer.

Learn the check list points and remember to use them as a help in your exam.

Your LO2 answer should contain	yes	no
three different points selected from the source. relevant selected points. explanations of what your selected quotes mean. at least two different pieces of recalled information. accurate recalled information. detailed recalled information. relevant recalled information.		

If you have ticked yes to everything then your answer is good. If you have ticked a 'no' make sure that part of your answer is improved.

Here is an example of an LO2 question from 'Wallace, Bruce and the Wars of Independence, 1286–1328'.

Source A: written about the succession of the Maid of Norway.

Alexander III's sudden death in March 1286 was especially tragic because all his children had died before him. His only living descendant was his granddaughter, Margaret, known as the Maid of Norway. Alexander had forced the Scottish nobility to accept Margaret as his heir although they do not appear to have been enthusiastic. They were worried she could not lead an army into battle and they would need to find her a husband.

Question: Why did the succession of the Maid cause problems for the Scots?
(Use **Source A** and recall.) (5 marks)

You should put into your own words points from the source such as:

1 The Scottish nobles had been forced to accept Margaret as the future queen.
2 They were worried that Margaret could not lead the army into battle like earlier kings had done.
3 They were worried that they would have to find a suitable husband for Margaret.
4 The husband of Margaret might interfere in the running of Scotland and he might try to control the Scottish queen.

BUT REMEMBER – IT IS NEVER ENOUGH ONLY TO WRITE SENTENCES FROM THE SOURCE.

If you do quote, you must develop or put into your own words what the quotes mean.

For example, you should explain that the Guardians of Scotland had agreed Margaret would be queen simply because there was no other descendant of Alexander left alive. She was next in the royal line.

You must also use recall. For example, you could write about Margaret being too young and living in Norway when her grandfather, Alexander III, died.

You should be aware that Edward I saw a chance to increase his power over the young queen and even wanted to marry his son to Margaret. The nobles were, therefore, worried that Scotland might lose its independence.

Finally, there was a fear that Scottish nobles might try to grab power for themselves so there was a danger of civil war.

Now try to write a good answer using the self-check marking guide and the advice just given – but try not to look back and just copy the points mentioned.

How did you get on?

Remember to give yourself a mark for each explained point from the source up to a maximum of three. Then give two marks for recall – one for each piece of relevant and accurate information.

You could get five marks for this question.

Here is an example from 'From the Cradle to the Grave? Social Welfare in Britain, 1890s–1951'.

Source B: written by a modern historian.

> The Second World War had a huge impact on the home front. A number of welfare reforms, such as the introduction of a Family Allowances Scheme, took place during the war. The suffering of the people during the war made them determined to create a better society after the war. The Government took a much greater role in helping people. The British public expected their Government to do more for them.

Question: 'Why did the Second World War encourage demands for improved social welfare?' (Use **Source B** and recall.)

Example

This model answer shows one way to combine source information along with recall to explain and develop the points in the source.

'The source states that "the suffering of the people made them determined to create a better society after the war" (from source). They "expected their Government to do more for them" (from source).

During the war bombing had destroyed many thousands of houses (from recall and development of source) which would need to be replaced by better homes. Evacuation from target areas usually involved children from poorer areas being sent away from industrial

Example continued ➤

Example *continued*

areas that were often places of bad housing and poverty to rural better-off places (from recall and development of source). People who took in evacuees became more aware of the problem of poverty (from recall).

During the war the government took greater control over people's lives (source). For example, rationing tried to make sure that every one had fair shares of food, clothing and fuel (from recall). When the war ended the people wanted the government to continue making Britain a better place than it had been before the war (reference to question) by tackling the social problems identified by the Beveridge Report which was written during the war (recall).'

 Remember when you are using information from the source do not copy out whole sentences from the source only.

The advice from the SQA is that you should put the evidence from the source in your own words – or if you do copy out phrases or sentences you must make it clear why you have selected them.

Here is an example of an LO2 question from 'The Road to War, 1933–1939'.

Source A: explains why Chamberlain followed a policy of appeasement.

> The Treaty that ended the First World War left Germany a bitter nation. Politicians at the time felt that as long as Germany felt like that then there would never be a lasting peace in Europe.
>
> Chamberlain agreed with this opinion and took a favourable view of Hitler's complaints about how Germany had been treated after the war. He knew the peace had been dictated and he believed that if Germany's complaints were dealt with fairly then peace in Europe would last.

Question: Why did Chamberlain decide to follow a policy of appeasement?
(Use **Source A** and recall.) (5 marks)

Hints *and* **Tips**

A good way to lay out an answer is to write a separate sentence about each point taken from the source and also include recall. Break your points into different paragraphs.

Example

'Chamberlain decided to follow appeasement for several reasons.

He knew that after the First World War Germany had been left "a bitter nation" and wanted to tear up the Treaty of Versailles and also wanted revenge (from source). Appeasement was a way of sorting out problems caused by the treaty. (point 1)

Example *continued* ➤

Example *continued*

Chamberlain knew that if Germany wanted revenge there "would never be lasting peace in Europe". Appeasement was a way of removing possible causes for war such as allowing Germany to remilitarise the Rhineland (from source plus recall). (point 2)

Chamberlain knew that the peace treaty "had been dictated" which means Germany had no voice in the treaty (from source extract and explained) and Hitler used that excuse to claim that Germany had been badly treated. (point 3)

Chamberlain believed that if Germany's complaints could be sorted out by negotiation then war would be avoided. These complaints were about Germany's loss of land, loss of population and the cuts in its military strength at the end of the First World War (from recall). (point 4)

There were also other reasons why Chamberlain followed appeasement. For example he was advised that Britain was not strong enough to fight Germany.

He also knew that Britain was more concerned with protecting its empire.

In a future war Britain might have to fight with no allies and that might mean defeat for Britain.

Chamberlain was also concerned that in a war there would be millions of civilian casualties as "the bomber would always get through", dropping gas bombs on British cities (all from recall).

In conclusion Chamberlain followed appeasement partly because he thought it was right to sort out Germany's complaints and also necessary to avoid getting involved in a war again.'

Why is this a good answer?

There is a clear introduction, development and conclusion.

The introduction is very brief but the candidate is aware that there is a lot to write about in a limited time and gets on with it.

The source is used fully and points made in the source are developed well.

There is a lot of relevant and detailed recall and overall this candidate has answered the question asked fully.

LO3 questions

What does evaluate mean?

Evaluate means to judge a source as evidence for finding out about something. In LO3 questions it is never enough just to describe what is in a source.

It might be helpful to understand what is needed in this sort of question by asking yourself the following questions about a source.

1   WHO produced the source? Is that relevant in assessing the value of a source?

2   WHAT is in the source and how is that relevant to the question?

3 WHEN was the source produced and how might that help in the evaluation of the source?

4 WHY was the source produced? What did the person who produced the source want to achieve?

How do I spot an evaluation question?

You will get an evaluation question in each of the three contexts you are answering. You can usually spot them because they ask questions which have the words and phrases in them such as, 'how useful', 'how reliable' or 'how valuable' (refer to Chapter 1 to make sure you know what these words mean).

You will also be asked to COMPARE two sources and you might also be asked to write a BALANCED answer.

You can find out more about these types of questions later in this chapter.

What is meant by a balanced answer?

In any evaluation question, the sources will seldom be entirely valuable or useful but they will NEVER be useless. They will have limitations and it's up to you to explain what these limits to usefulness are. In this case, a useful word to use is PARTLY! By answering that a source is partly useful you have the chance to explain why the source is useful but you should also explain why the source might not give the whole story. You should also include relevant information from your own knowledge which further helps to evaluate the source.

Must I use my own knowledge as well as the source content?

Yes! In this sort of question recalled knowledge is really important.

To evaluate historical sources you are expected to write about the source's ORIGIN and PURPOSE. You must also place the source in its CONTEXT. All these words are defined in Chapter 1.

When dealing with origin, you should also be careful about simply writing down information from the source. The question paper will give you information about where the source comes from but it is up to you to use that information to help explain why the source might be useful.

For example, if a source was by Churchill, a politician in the 1930s who was against appeasement, you will not get marks just for writing that the source was written by Winston Churchill. What you should do is show off your knowledge and give more information by writing, 'the source was written by Churchill, a leading opponent of appeasement whose view was in the minority for most of the 1930s'.

You should also make clear that you know if a source is primary or secondary but again you will not get marks for doing just that. For example, if you had an extract from Martin Luther King's 'I have a dream' speech you should write 'the source is a primary source broadcast live on national television when a huge demonstration took place in Washington in 1963'. By doing this, you are showing knowledge and developing your point.

You could also explain the importance of the person making the speech, for example 'Martin Luther King was the main leader of the Civil Rights Movement whose speeches inspired protesters and demonstrators to change racist laws in the USA in the 1950s and 60s'.

You should also mention why the source was written (in other words its purpose). That will help you to judge how useful or reliable or how biased a source might be. Using the example of the 'dream' speech you could write, 'This source was part of a speech which was intended to gain more publicity for the Civil Rights Movement and put pressure on the US government to pass the Civil Rights Act'.

Finally, if the source is a secondary source you should write something like this – 'a secondary source written with the benefit of hindsight'. You could also assume a secondary source is likely to be more balanced and possibly more detailed.

It is more likely to be factually correct because it was written after the event giving the author time to check information.

It is LESS likely to be biased because the writer is less personally involved so less likely to take sides unfairly.

As you study the examples in this section think how they fit into the LO3 mark grid.

Use this grid to self-check your LO3 answers in Chapter 14.

As the grid reminds you, when you check off every point on the list you can be confident you have a good answer.

Learn the check list points and remember to use them as a help in your exam.

Your LO3 answer should	yes	no
briefly explain the context in which the source was produced. evaluate by commenting on origin. evaluate by commenting on possible purpose. select words and phrases from source to support your evaluation. identify bias by giving examples if there are any. include accurate recalled information. include relevant recalled information. end with a balanced conclusion which answers the question asked.		

If you have ticked yes to everything then your answer is good. If you have ticked a 'no' make sure that that part of your answer is improved.

Now try this example from 'The Road to War, 1933–1939'.

Source B: from a German newspaper sold on 28 June 1919.

> Vengeance!
>
> German nation!
>
> Today in the Hall of Mirrors at Versailles a disgraceful treaty is being signed. Never forget it! Today German honour is dragged to the grave. Never forget it! The German people will push forward to reconquer their place among the nations of the world. There will be vengeance for the shame of 1919.

Question: How useful is **Source B** for finding out about German foreign policy in the 1930s? (4 marks)

Example

Here is a weak answer to the question:

'This source is useful because it refers to revenge for the Treaty of Versailles. Hitler wanted to destroy the Treaty of Versailles which is called "the shame of 1919". It refers to the disgrace caused by the treaty and says, "German honour is dragged to the grave". It shows German policy was aggressive because it says Germans must "reconquer their place" and "There will be vengeance".'

Why is this a weak answer?

This source is weak mainly because it really just describes the source.

It does not evaluate the source.

It does not mention the origin, the purpose or even the authorship of the source.

It claims that German policy was aggressive but uses very little recall to support that view.

There is no conclusion providing a balanced answer.

This answer has not done enough to pass.

Example

Here is a much better answer:

'This source is partly useful for finding out about German foreign policy in the 1930s.

The source is from a German newspaper which is angry about the Treaty of Versailles which had just been signed. It uses phrases and words such as "German honour being dragged to the grave" and a "disgraceful" treaty. Germans were shocked and horrified by the Treaty which punished Germany for starting World War One. They wanted revenge on those countries that forced Germany to sign the treaty. In the 1930s most of Hitler's foreign policy was aimed at breaking the treaty.

Example continued ➤

Example continued

Overall the source is not very useful for finding out about German foreign policy in the 1930s. It does not mention remilitarising the Rhineland, Anschluss, the Czech crisis or the invasion of Poland.

All these things in some way broke the Treaty of Versailles.

The source gives the background to German foreign policy but no detail of that policy.'

Why is this a much better answer?

This answer is much better because it evaluates the source by referring to the origins and possible purpose of the source. It links the answer back to the original question several times. It uses a lot of recall to show knowledge of policy in the 1930s and how that was linked to the treaty.

It reaches a balanced conclusion that correctly explains why the source is only of limited use for finding out about German foreign policy in the 1930s.

Remember

You never get sources that are entirely useless!

Don't just describe the source – that's not evaluating!

Make sure your answer refers to all the advice points provided with the question.

Provide a balanced answer that includes your own knowledge.

Make sure your evaluation does what you are asked to do in the question.

Hints and Tips

If you think a source is biased prove it!

You will not get marks just for writing that a source is biased. You must identify the examples of bias in the source and then prove you know what bias is by writing about the example you are giving. Always provide evidence of the bias in your answer by quoting and explaining.

Never reject a source with bias as useless or not valuable. A biased source is how someone felt about something and always gives a point of view. Yes it will be one sided but as long as you point that out in your answer you will gain marks for saying so.

Evaluating picture questions

In recent years, illustrations such as pictures, cartoons and posters have all been used in the exam paper.

How should I answer picture-based questions?

An illustration or cartoon or drawing starts life as an idea. The artist, cartoonist or even photographer then uses their ideas to produce the illustration. But what gives them the idea? What events happened which caused the artists to think as they did and caused the illustration to be produced?

The secret of a good answer to 'a picture question' lies in knowing what the illustration is about and what point of view the artist has about the event.

Here is an example from 'From the Cradle to the Grave? Social Welfare in Britain, 1890s–1951'.

Source A: from a government poster published in 1911 advertising one of the social reforms of the Liberals.

The right ticket for you

Question: How useful is **Source A** as evidence of the social reforms of the Liberals? (4 marks)

How do I know what event the illustration is about?

Every source in the exam comes with a brief introduction outlining where the source comes from and when it was produced. This information is always useful in letting you know what the source is about. For example, in the example above, you are told it is from a government poster published in 1911 and the question mentions the social reforms of the Liberals. You will always be given enough information about an illustration to decide what it is about.

Example

Here is a weak answer to the 'Cradle to Grave' poster shown earlier:

'The poster shows a hand holding a ticket called "the right ticket for you". It refers to a safe return which workers got during illness. For paying out 4d a male worker got in return 10 shillings a week for 26 weeks and also a free doctor and medicine.'

Why is this a weak answer?

Although the answer includes a lot of detail from the poster there is no direct answer to the question set. There is no attempt to evaluate or even place the poster in context.

There is no recall.

This answer risks gaining no marks.

How should a good answer be constructed?

Follow these steps to answer any cartoon/illustration question.

1   Check the date: It is 1911. The question asks about the Liberal reforms so that should tell you the poster is about the National Insurance scheme introduced by the Liberals at that time.

2   Check the source: It is a government poster so likely to give a positive impression of the reform.

3   Check the details in the poster. It provides details of the cost and benefits of the new insurance scheme.

Example

Here is a much better answer:

'The poster is partly useful for finding out about the social reforms of the Liberals.

In 1911 the Liberal Government introduced a new National Insurance scheme. Part of the scheme helped unemployed men but the part shown in the poster was health insurance. By paying 4d a week into the scheme a male worker was entitled to 10 shillings a week when off sick for up to 26 weeks. The insured person also got free treatment by a doctor and free medicine. The scheme was often called 9d for 4d because the employer and government also contributed.

For many workers this reform was a huge help so it did seem that it was the right ticket for workers and gave them a "safe return".

The poster is very useful evidence of the National Insurance scheme that helped sick workers but is no use at all for finding out about the other social reforms of the Liberals such as Old Age Pensions or reforms to help children.'

Why is this a good answer?

The answer starts by providing an overall answer to the question which is then developed.

There is a scene-setting introduction that contains recall.

The answer not only describes the content of the poster but also links it to the Liberal reforms.

Finally, there is a balanced evaluation that directly answers the question.

Here is an example from 'Free at Last? Race Relations in the USA, 1918–1968'.

Source B: from a 1930s poster advertising the benefits of living in the USA.

World's highest standard of living

Question: How useful is **Source B** as evidence of the experience of immigrants to the USA in the 1920s and 1930s? (4 marks)

Must I use my own knowledge in this answer?

Yes. It is never enough just to describe what you see in the illustration. You MUST use your own knowledge to explain in detail the points shown or hinted at in the illustration.

Write an answer long enough to make as many developed points as there are marks for the question.

Example

Here is a weak answer:

'The cartoon is from the 1930s. It shows a happy American family driving a car. Above the car is a sign saying "world's highest standard of living". Many immigrants went to America looking for a good life and this family have found it. The poster is quite useful as evidence of the experience of many immigrants to the USA.'

Why is this a weak answer?

There is very little scene-setting introduction.

This answer picks on certain features in the poster but fails to explain them fully.

There is almost no recall apart from stating why some people migrated to the USA.

There is only a very slight attempt at evaluation in the answer – 'the poster is quite useful as evidence'.

Example

A much better answer would be like this:

'Many immigrants travelled to America in the early 20th century. They hoped to find a better life and the poster shows that some have found it.

The family in the car might be immigrants who are successful but they are clearly WASPS and these white Anglo Saxons often did do well in the USA. They agreed there was no way like the American way. The same was not true for other groups. Many immigrants from south and east Europe were persecuted or discriminated against because of the colour of their skin or their political beliefs. They found it difficult to adjust to the "American way". Most immigrants were poor and lived in poor housing at first. However all immigrants wanted to believe the poster. They hoped to find the American Dream.

Overall this poster is quite useful in showing what immigrants would like to become but is not useful in showing what many had to face in the 1920s and 30s.

Why is this a good answer?

There is a brief introduction which outlines why so many people migrated to the USA.

The answer uses the content of the cartoon and also uses recalled information. The answer also includes a good connection between what immigrants wanted to find in America and the reality that they did find.

Finally there is a direct answer to the question.

Hints *and* Tips

Don't ignore the illustration. Use the information about who produced it and when and where to help you explain why it was produced.

Don't just describe the illustration. Explain the point being made by the producer of the illustration. What thoughts or emotions did the producer want to stir in the people who saw the illustration?

Finally do what you are asked to do. Link the illustration to the main point of the question by doing the evaluation asked in the question.

Here is another example from 'Free at Last? Race Relations in the USA, 1918–1968'.

Source A: shows members of the Ku Klux Klan marching in Washington DC in 1926.

Ku Klux Klan

Question: How useful is **Source A** as evidence of the activities of the Ku Klux Klan between the First and Second World Wars? (4 marks)

Use your LO3 grid to decide what this answer should get

Here are suggestions that should be made in an answer.

'The source is partly useful as evidence of the activities of the Ku Klux Klan between the First and Second World Wars. The photograph is a primary source showing a Klan march in 1926 so it does show an activity between the First and Second World Wars.

It also shows the Klan as a patriotic organisation carrying the flag of the USA. The Klan is also shown marching in Washington DC near the centre of US government. This shows that the KKK must have been a respected organisation at the time. In the 1920s the new KKK became strong under the slogan "America for Americans" and "100% Americanism".'

On the other hand, the source does not show the bad side of Klan activities such as terrorising Black people, lynchings or cross burnings.

This source gives a one-sided positive image of an orderly, peaceful organisation so it is only partly useful as evidence of Klan activities between the wars.'

The comparison question

Am I likely to be asked a comparison question?

You will always get a question that asks you to compare two sources in your exam.

How do I spot a comparison question?

Sometimes the question will obviously be a comparison question because it will use the word 'compare' in the question such as 'Compare the views of sources B and C on the National Health Service'.

Compare questions can also be slightly disguised when the word compare does NOT appear in the question. However, they are easy to spot because they are the only question you will be doing that will refer to TWO sources in the question – such as 'To what extent do sources C and D agree about…'.

What does compare mean?

A comparison question asks you to make clear connections between sources. The skill being assessed is your ability to compare and that does not mean your ability to describe two sources.

Suppose you were asked to compare the two girls in the drawing.

Girl A

Girl B

Two girls

Example

Here is a very weak answer that would probably gain no marks:

'Girl A has long blonde hair. She is skinny. She has a light coloured top on and a short skirt. She has matching shoes and is tall. Girl B has dark curly hair. She is plump. She is wearing a dark top and baggy trousers. She is not very tall.'

Why is this a weak answer?

Simply because it does not answer the question. The answer just provides a description of each girl. There is no comparison.

Example

A much better answer would be:

'Overall, A and B are quite different although there is one similarity. They are both girls.

Girl A has long blonde hair but girl B has dark curly hair.

Girl A is much skinnier than girl B.

The clothes they wear are also different. A is wearing a light coloured top with a short skirt and matching shoes whereas B has on a dark top and baggy trousers which hide her footwear.'

Why is this a much better answer?

In this answer there are at least FIVE points of comparison involving gender, hair, body shape, clothes and shoes.

What are examiners looking for?

The SQA advice on this sort of question is very clear: 'In comparison questions specific comparisons must be made. Exam candidates will not gain marks for writing "Source A says…" and then "Source B says…".'

If you want a good mark, it is not enough just to quote a sentence from one source then quote from another. By all means do that as part of your answer but you should also explain the point you are making by using your own words. That is what is meant by a developed comparison.

If you are asked to 'compare the evidence' then it is correct to compare the origin as well as the content of the sources.

If you are asked 'how far…' or 'to what extent do the sources agree…' then you should only compare the content of the sources.

If you are asked how far the sources agree or disagree, make a decision then give examples from the sources to support your decision. You will usually find there are some points where the sources agree and other points where they disagree.

Here is an example of a comparison question from 'From the Cradle to Grave? Social Welfare in Britain, 1890s–1951'.

Source B: from a speech by the Health Minister in 1946.

> This new law will give us a free universal health service with no insurance qualifications of any sort. We do not intend to limit the amount of help given. There will be a service of local doctors, specialists, hospitals, eye treatment, dental treatment and hearing facilities.

Source C: from a book by a modern historian.

> The service that emerged was paid for very largely by taxes. There was a flood of people seeking treatment. Prescriptions cost twice the figure they had before. Dentists had expected about four million patients a year but twice that number wanted treatment. The National Health Service became too expensive and by 1951 it had to introduce charges.

Question: Compare the views of **Sources B** and **C** on the National Health Service. (4 marks)

Example

Here is a good answer:

'Source B is a primary source from a member of the government. It is a speech made to show the good points of the Health Service that the government is trying to create.

On the other hand source C is from a secondary source written with the benefit of hindsight and providing a more realistic assessment of what really happened when the NHS started. (First mark)

The sources disagree about the cost of the new service. B claims it will be free but C writes that the costs of the service were "paid for very largely by taxes". C also claims that "Prescriptions cost twice the figure they had before". Source C then goes on to write that by 1951 the "NHS had become too expensive" and some charges had to be introduced to pay for the services. (Second mark)

The sources also disagree over the level of demand for services. Source B believed there would be no limit to the amount of help given but C knew that there was a "flood of people seeking treatment" which the government could not cope with without making charges for some services. (Third mark)

In conclusion source B is looking to the future and trying to promote the government's new idea of a NHS while source C is a more realistic look back at what really happened.' (Fourth mark)

Why is this a good answer?

This answer is good because it compares the sources point by point.

There are enough comparison points made to gain full marks. (In this example the places where marks are gained are shown.)

The points from the sources are not just quoted, they are explained and developed in the answer.

There is an overall conclusion that shows understanding of the main point of each source.

Here is a second example from 'Wallace, Bruce and the Wars of Independence 1286–1328'.

Source B: describes what happened after the battle of Falkirk. It was written by a Scottish chronicler, John of Fordun, in the 1370s.

After the English won the Battle of Falkirk through the treachery of some Scots, William Wallace realised the obvious wickedness of the Comyns and their friends. He decided to serve with the ordinary people rather than to be set over them. Therefore he resigned as Guardian'.

Source C: describes what happened after the Battle of Falkirk. It was written by a modern Scottish historian in the 1970s.

> William Wallace escaped from the Battle of Falkirk with his life but his power was shattered. Wallace came from a social class that had not been involved in ruling Scotland. His rivals resented the fact that he was only a common man and not a noble. When Wallace was defeated and fell from power, more traditional leaders took over again.

Question: Compare the reasons for Wallace's resignation as Guardian given in **Sources B** and **C**. (4 marks)

Source B claims that Wallace resigned because he did not trust some of the Scottish nobles. Fordun wrote, 'Wallace realised the obvious wickedness of the Comyns and their friends'. On the other hand **Source C** suggests Wallace resigned because the Scottish nobles did not like him not being a nobleman.

Example

Here is a good answer:

'Fordun suggests that Wallace resigned because he felt he would be happier working and fighting with the ordinary people rather than ruling them. However source C blames Wallace's resignation on the defeat at Falkirk that shattered his power.

In conclusion source B thinks that Wallace chose to resign but source C believes he was forced to resign after his defeat because he had no support left and was disliked by Scotland's "more traditional leaders".'

Why is this a much better answer?

This answer is good because it compares the sources point by point.

There are enough comparison points made to gain full marks.

The points from the sources are not just quoted, they are explained and developed in the answer.

There is an overall conclusion that shows understanding of the main point of each source.

SECTION 2

What you must know – *THE CONTENT GUIDES*

Now you know HOW to answer the questions, all you have to do is be sure of the subject content. You will have notes and books that provide you with all the detailed content you need so the next section of this book will only provide content outlines, focusing on what you really need to know about each of the eight most popular topics.

Each part will provide you with FOUR main things. These are:

◆ A list of key points based on the Intermediate 2 syllabus which tells you what you must be able to do.

◆ Essential information for each part of the syllabus.

◆ Advice on the most likely issues you will be asked about and also anything you should watch out for.

◆ Exam question practice with self-check answers.

Chapter 6

SCOTTISH AND BRITISH, CONTEXT 2: WALLACE, BRUCE AND THE WARS OF INDEPENDENCE, 1286–1328

The first part of the syllabus is about Scotland between 1286 and 1296.

Key Points

You must be able to:

◆ Explain why the death of Margaret left Scotland with a serious problem.

◆ Explain why civil war was a possibility in Scotland.

◆ Explain why the Scots appealed to Edward I of England for help.

◆ Describe how Edward tried to increase his power over Scotland peacefully.

Scotland between 1286 and 1296

In 1286, King Alexander III of Scotland fell from his horse and was killed. The next in line to the throne was Alexander's granddaughter Margaret. She was to be the next Queen but she was only a child and lived in Norway.

The important noblemen in Scotland decided to ask King Edward I of England to help them decide who would rule Scotland until Margaret was old enough to rule on her own.

Edward wanted to help but first of all he wanted the Scots to accept him as Overlord of Scotland. That meant he would be in complete charge of Scotland. Second, he wanted his son, Prince Edward, to marry Princess Margaret. That would mean that any child of the marriage would rule both Scotland and England. Scotland would in effect become absorbed by England. However, when Margaret sailed to Scotland she took ill on the journey and died. Scotland was left with no clear leader and ambitious nobles in Scotland saw their chance to seize power. To prevent a civil war in Scotland, King Edward I of England was asked to be an independent judge and decide who should be the next king of Scotland.

The second part of the syllabus is about the Great Cause.

Key Points

You must be able to:

- Explain what 'the Great Cause' means.
- Explain why the Scots did not want to accept Edward as Overlord.
- Explain why John Balliol and the Bruce family both believed they had a good claim to the throne of Scotland.
- Explain why Edward chose Balliol to be Scottish king.

The Great Cause

The Great Cause was the legal struggle to choose a new king of Scotland. The Scots argued that nobody in Scotland had the right to choose a king. They argued that God alone had that right. However, they agreed that another king could also make that decision. As a result, the Scots asked Edward I of England to decide between all the claimants. Edward said he would only choose a leader who accepted him as Overlord. At first the Scots refused but then agreed to Edward's terms.

There were fourteen nobles who claimed the right to be Scotland's next king although there were really only a few who had a strong claim.

Edward chose John Balliol as the next Scottish king. This decision angered the Bruce family who thought they had the best claim to the throne.

Balliol was crowned King of Scotland on 30 November 1292. Edward believed he could control Balliol and interfere in Scotland whenever he wanted to.

The third part of the syllabus is about the reign of King John Balliol.

Key Points

You must be able to:

- Describe how Edward tried to control Balliol.
- Explain why Balliol is thought of as a weak king.
- Explain why war broke out between Scotland and England.
- Describe Edward's invasion of Scotland and how he established control over Scotland.

King John Balliol

King John Balliol did not have an easy time. Edward insisted that King John had to obey him. Edward often overruled many of Balliol's decisions in Scotland. Edward even refused to accept that Scotland was an independent country.

King Edward invades Scotland

When England went to war with France, Edward wanted Scots to fight in the English army. The Scots refused and made an alliance with France. Edward became even more angry when the Scots launched an attack into England. Edward retaliated by invading Scotland, almost destroying the important Scottish port of Berwick-upon-Tweed. Edward then advanced into Scotland, defeating the Scottish army at Dunbar and eventually capturing King John. Edward then tried to destroy Scotland's identity and independence. He removed important symbols of Scottish independence such as the Stone of Destiny. The English army occupied Scotland's castles and English governors were put in charge of Scotland.

 ## *The next part of the syllabus is about William Wallace.*

Key Points

You must be able to:

- ◆ Explain why Wallace led a rebellion against the English.
- ◆ Describe Wallace's victory at Stirling Bridge.
- ◆ Explain the effect Wallace's defeat had on Scotland.
- ◆ Explain why Wallace was defeated at Falkirk.
- ◆ Describe the capture and execution of Wallace.

By the summer of 1297, many Scots were starting to fight back against the English occupation.

Stirling Bridge

William Wallace and Andrew Murray became famous throughout Scotland because of their attacks on the English. Edward decided to send an army to crush the Scots. The armies met at Stirling Bridge.

Although the English army was much bigger than the Scottish army, Wallace ordered the Scots to attack when the English army was struggling to cross the bridge over the River Forth. The English were defeated and as a reward Wallace was made the official Guardian of Scotland.

The Battle of Falkirk

But Wallace had enemies. Some nobles were jealous of his rise to power, especially as Wallace was not a nobleman. Wallace also said he fought for King John Balliol and that annoyed the Bruce family. Most importantly King Edward of England was determined to take back power in Scotland.

At Falkirk, in July 1298, a new English army destroyed the Scots and Wallace's reputation as a great Scottish leader was gone.

Public execution

In 1304, Wallace was captured near Glasgow and taken to London as a traitor where he was executed publicly and horribly. King Edward believed that by making an example of Wallace other Scots would be too scared to fight the English.

➡ *The next part of the syllabus is about Robert Bruce from 1306 up to the Battle of Bannockburn in 1314.*

Key Points

You must be able to:

◆ Describe how Robert the Bruce became king.

◆ Describe how Bruce defeated his enemies in Scotland.

◆ Describe how Bruce defeated the English.

◆ Explain why Bruce was successful in defeating his enemies.

◆ Describe the Battle of Bannockburn.

How did Robert the Bruce become king?

Robert the Bruce wanted to be king but Bruce had a rival called John Comyn.

In 1305, Comyn and Bruce met in Greyfriars Monastery, Dumfries – and only Bruce came out alive!

Bruce was blamed for the murder. The powerful relatives and supporters of Comyn were determined to get revenge and Edward I ordered that Bruce was to be captured and executed.

Bruce decided that his only hope was to make himself king, gather support, defeat Comyn's friends and also push the English out of Scotland! But things started badly for Bruce.

How did Robert the Bruce defeat his enemies?

Soon after Bruce became king his supporters were defeated and Bruce was on the run. He used hit and run tactics and ambushes to surprise his enemies. Slowly Bruce built up his strength and hit back.

By 1314 Stirling Castle was the last Scottish castle still controlled by the English

Once Bruce had defeated the Comyn family's supporters he concentrated on pushing the English out of Scotland. Slowly Bruce recaptured Scotland's castles and by 1314 only Stirling Castle was still controlled by the English.

King Edward I had died but his son, Edward II, still wanted to control Scotland. Luckily for Bruce, Edward II did not have his father's ability as a military leader or politician.

The Battle of Bannockburn

In 1314, Edward sent a very large army into Scotland to save Stirling Castle. Bruce knew he had to defeat the whole English army and chose to fight at Bannockburn, on the road to nearby Stirling.

In June 1314, the Scots defeated the huge English army. England no longer had power over Scotland but Scotland was not yet a free country.

This part of the syllabus is about the reign of King Robert I.

Key Points

You must be able to:

◆ Describe how King Robert kept his authority over the Scots noblemen.

◆ Explain why the Declaration of Arbroath was a very important document.

◆ Explain why even today Scots think that the Declaration of Arbroath is a very important document.

◆ Describe how Scotland became a free and independent nation again.

King Robert I

After the Battle of Bannockburn, Robert the Bruce was recognised by all Scots as Robert I, King of Scots. Bruce gave lands and power to his most trusted and loyal supporters. Scottish nobles were forced to give up their estates in England so that they would have no obligations to the English king.

The Scots launched raids into the north of England but still the king, Edward II, would not accept Scottish independence.

The Declaration of Arbroath
In 1320, the Declaration of Arbroath was written. It was a document sent to the Pope and signed by Scottish noblemen. It asked the Pope to recognise Scotland as a free country and to accept Bruce as Scotland's proper king.

The Treaty of Edinburgh
Finally, in 1328, the Treaty of Edinburgh (also called the Treaty of Northampton) was agreed between Scotland and England. Bruce was recognised as King of Scots and Scotland was a free and independent country again.

Now practise your skills

The next two questions are examples of the types of questions you can expect in this section.

You will find model answers in Chapter 14.

The answers provided have two purposes.

◆   First, they show examples of good answers to the question.
◆   Second, they provide more information on the topic.

Questions

LO1

Question: Describe the methods used by King Edward to take control of Scotland after the defeat of John Balliol. (5 marks)

LO3

Source A: part of a letter from supporters of Robert Bruce to John Comyn in 1290.

> Although Robert Bruce is the true heir of Scotland, you and your supporters want to make John Balliol king. Therefore, because of this unfairness, we appeal to King Edward of England to assist Robert Bruce in obtaining what is his right.

Question: How reliable is **Source A** as evidence of disagreements in Scotland about who should be King of Scots? (4 marks)

Chapter 7

SCOTTISH AND BRITISH, CONTEXT 6: IMMIGRANTS AND EXILES: SCOTLAND, 1830s–1930s

The first part of the syllabus is about the why so many Irish migrated to Scotland after 1830.

Key Points

You must be able to:

◆ Describe living and working conditions for most Irish people in Ireland around 1830.

◆ Describe the problems in Ireland caused by the potato blight.

◆ Explain why so many Irish migrated to central Scotland.

Reasons for the Irish migration to Scotland

In 1830, all of Ireland was part of Britain.

Most of the Irish population was poor and Catholic. They usually worked on farms and survived on a diet of milk and potatoes. Housing was bad, unemployment was common and most of the population lived and died in poverty.

In the 1840s, disaster happened when a potato disease destroyed the crop, year after year. Almost two million people died of starvation or illness. Another two million emigrated to escape the famine. Most went to mainland Britain, landing at ports such as Liverpool or Glasgow.

Central Scotland

Irish immigrants in Scotland often settled in the West of Scotland around Glasgow. There were thousands of jobs in the new growing industries such as cotton factories, coal mines, ironworks and shipbuilding. Other Scottish cities also attracted Irish migrants. Living and working conditions in the industrial cities and factories of Scotland were hard but better than the life left behind in Ireland.

The next part of the syllabus is about the living and working conditions of Irish immigrants in Scotland.

Key Points

You must be able to:

◆ Describe the living conditions of Irish immigrants in Scotland.

◆ Explain why many Scots did not like Irish immigrants.

◆ Describe ways the Irish immigrants kept alive their own identity in Scotland.

Irish living conditions in Scotland

In the mid-nineteenth century, Scotland's industrial towns and cities were overcrowded, dirty and full of diseases.

Irish emigrants were poor and could only afford to live in the cheapest and poorest areas of these industrial towns and cities of central Scotland. The local Scots were no better off but resented the Irish immigrants who now competed for housing and jobs. Soon the Irish settlers were being blamed for causing the problems. The Scots argued that because immigrants increased the demand for housing and jobs, rents were kept high and wages were kept low.

Religion was also an issue. Many of the Irish immigrants were Catholic but the population of central Scotland was mostly Protestant.

The Catholic Church worked hard to provide education and help for the new families settling in Scotland. The Church also provided social and sporting clubs where Irish migrants could relax and keep alive their religious and cultural habits from 'the old country'.

Scottish reaction to the Irish emigrants

The mainly Protestant Scots were suspicious of the immigrants who kept themselves to themselves. The Orange Lodge was an organisation started to protect Protestant identity which members claimed was being threatened by Catholic immigration. Football clubs were and are examples of the sectarian divide in Scotland with Catholic Celtic facing Protestant Rangers in Glasgow and Hibernian and Hearts in Edinburgh showing the same split in the population.

Between 1830 and 1930, anti-Irish and anti-Catholic feelings were stirred up in newspapers and books which claimed that the Irish were 'an inferior race'.

For many years, the Irish faced discrimination in employment because they were Catholic but as the years went by Scots and Irish intermarried and many Scots today have Irish ancestors.

The next part of the syllabus is about emigration from the Highlands of Scotland.

Key Points

You must be able to:

◆ Explain what is meant by 'push' and 'pull' reasons for emigration.
◆ Describe the problems facing Highland Scots in the mid-nineteenth century.
◆ Describe what was done to help Scots emigrate.

'Push' and 'pull'

Between 1830 and 1930, it has been estimated that over two million people left Scotland, either for 'push' reasons or 'pull' reasons.

In the Highlands, 'push' reasons included eviction to make way for more profitable sheep farms or later to make way for tourism which often involved grouse shooting or deer stalking. Over-population was also a problem. There were too many people trying to make a living on too little fertile land. Most families lived in small, dark, dirty cottages. Wages were very low. Work was scarce. The potato blight, a disease that destroyed potatoes, affected the Highlands as well as Ireland.

On the other hand, many Highlanders chose to emigrate in search of opportunities. These 'pull' reasons included incentives such as promises of cheap land, travelling expenses paid for and the hope of a better life, either in the Lowlands or abroad – even England!

Migration from Scotland

In the 1850s, the Highland and Island Emigration Society raised money to help those people who were suffering during the potato famine. It helped send emigrants to Australia. The British and Canadian governments also started the Crofter Colonisation Scheme, which was intended to help people migrate from Scotland and settle on the Canadian prairies. These are only two examples of organisations created to help people migrate.

Thousands of Scots emigrated for both 'push' and 'pull' reasons

 The next part of the syllabus is about where Scots migrated to, the work they did and the contribution of individual Scots such as Andrew Carnegie.

Key Points

You must be able to:

- Describe ways in which Scots helped develop the new countries they went to.
- Describe ways that Scottish identity and culture have been kept alive around the world.
- Describe the work of some famous Scots who migrated.
- Explain why the emigration of Scots abroad was not always a good thing for local people.

Emigration from Scotland

Scots emigrated from both the Highlands and the Lowlands. They often went to countries that were part of the British Empire such as Canada, Australia and New Zealand.

Scots played an important part in developing the new lands where they settled. Scots soldiers, farmers, engineers and businessmen were all very important.

Scots took with them their customs and culture. Pipe bands, highland dress, highland games and Burns clubs appeared wherever Scots settled. Scottish music, songs and literature remained important to emigrants. Scottish place names are still common in Australasia and Canada.

Famous Scottish emigrants

Scots such as John Muir and Andrew Carnegie are examples of successful Scots emigrants. Carnegie, born in Dunfermline, Fife, made a fortune through hard work in the USA then spent most of it trying to help others both in the USA and in Scotland.

John Muir, born in Dunbar, East Lothian, was an environmentalist and conservationist long before these ideas became fashionable. He helped create Yellowstone National Park in the USA.

The effect of immigration on native peoples

However, Scots were also involved in things that would be disapproved off today. Many took land by force from the native peoples of North America and Australasia. These Scots were in turn doing to others what had been done to them. Native Americans, Aborigines and Maoris were cleared off their land to make way for immigrants. Ironically in Australasia the immigrants cleared land to make way for sheep farms.

Not all Scots were successful abroad. Many were unprepared for the reality of extreme weather, isolation and danger. Many Scots who emigrated returned to Scotland after a few years, but most returned only to the industrial cities of central Scotland and not to the highlands and islands from where they had come.

Now practise your skills

The next two questions are examples of the types of questions you can expect in this section.

You will find model answers in Chapter 14.

The answers provided have two purposes.

- ◆ First, they show examples of good answers to the question.
- ◆ Second, they provide more information on the topic.

Questions

LO2

Answer the following question using recalled knowledge and information from the sources where appropriate.

Source A: from an official report in 1836.

> A large number of Irish have arrived in Great Britain in recent years. The wages that they earn here are almost always higher than they could earn in their own country. Moreover the employment is more constant. They are able to obtain payment on a greater number of days in the year. There is more chance of getting employment for women and children in the manufacturing towns.

Question: Why did many Irish come to Scotland in the nineteenth century? (Use **Source A** and recall.) (5 marks)

LO3

Source B:

> Civilian emigration to Canada was encouraged by the problems caused to the crofters' way of life by improvements on Highland estates. It was also caused by the overpopulation of the area and crop failures. The Government established an Emigration Commission that issued advice to would-be emigrants.

Source C:

> For much of the nineteenth century emigration was seen as a solution to overpopulation in the Highlands. In the 1850s, funds were raised by the Highland and Island Emigration Society to relieve distress during the potato famine. It helped send emigrants to Australia. The British and Canadian governments set up the Crofter Colonisation Scheme, which was intended to reduce overpopulation in the crofting areas and to settle the Canadian prairies.

Question: How far do **Sources B** and **C** agree about emigration from Scotland? (5 marks)

SCOTTISH AND BRITISH CONTEXT 7(A): FROM THE CRADLE TO THE GRAVE? SOCIAL WELFARE IN BRITAIN, 1890s–1951

The first part of the syllabus is about the problem of poverty around 1900.

Key Points

You must be able to:

◆ Describe late nineteenth century attitudes towards poverty.

◆ Explain what 'self-help' meant.

◆ Explain why attitudes to poverty began to change by the early twentieth century.

Poverty in the late nineteenth century

Poverty was a huge social problem at the beginning of the twentieth century. Those who were not poor believed that poverty was caused by laziness, drunkenness or personal failure. Hard work and self-help were the best ways of avoiding poverty. Voluntary organisations existed to help the poor but there was no system of government help for the poor. Government policy at this time was called Laissez-Faire. It meant the government did not believe it was their job to help the poor.

Booth and Rowntree

By the early twentieth century attitudes to poverty were changing, partly because of two large investigations into poverty. In London, Charles Booth had researched poverty over many years and produced a huge report providing hard evidence that poverty had definite causes. In York, another investigation was carried out by Seebohm Rowntree.

The Booth and Rowntree reports showed that poverty was something individuals who were poor could not do much about. These reports were important in persuading the Liberal Government that came to power in 1906 to take action against poverty.

The wider effects of poverty

The Liberal Government was also concerned that poverty was weakening Britain. Army recruits were thought to be unfit. During the Boer War in South Africa many volunteers for the army were rejected as unfit for service. Politicians wondered if Britain would be strong enough to fight a bigger and better enemy in the future.

Another concern was that Britain was no longer a top industrial nation. It was clear that Britain needed healthier and better-educated workers. However, many children were thought to be too hungry and badly clothed to learn effectively.

Changing attitudes within the Liberal Party

Younger politicians within the Liberal Party were convinced the government should take more direct action in helping the poor. The Liberals were also concerned that the newly formed Labour Party would take votes away from the Liberals if Labour started to offer social reform.

These were the main reasons why the Liberals began to think about increased government action to help the poor and a decline in support for self-help.

The next part of the syllabus is about what the new Liberal Government did to help the poor between 1906 and 1914.

Key Points

You must be able to:

◆ Describe in some detail what the Liberals did to help the old, the young, the sick and the unemployed.

◆ Decide how successful the Liberal Reforms were.

Liberal reforms in the early twentieth century

The Liberal Reforms of 1906–1914 are very important because they marked the decline of the Laissez-Faire ideology and the acceptance of the idea that the government should have a large part to play in helping those who could not help themselves.

Between 1906 and 1914, the Liberal Reforms tried to deal with the problem of poverty and focused on four groups: the old, the young, the sick and the unemployed.

For the old, an old age pension was started for over 70s of good character.

For children, new laws called the Children's Charter tried to keep children away from alcohol and tobacco. School meals were started for some and medical inspections and treatments were also provided before 1914.

For the sick and unemployed, a new National Insurance Scheme was created which provided some unemployment benefit for some workers and some medical help for

Poverty and bad housing were problems that could not be solved by 'self-help'

HOW TO PASS INTERMEDIATE 2 HISTORY

insured workers. These insurance schemes were important as they combined contributions from the workers with money paid by the government and the employer. No longer did all workers have to rely on self-help during hard times.

Most people accepted that the reforms did help. However, pensions were only paid to over 70s and many poor died long before then.

Only a few industries were covered by unemployment insurance. Medical help was only provided to an insured worker and nothing was provided for other family members. Insurance contributions also cut into the already low wages of workers.

The next part of the syllabus is about how the government became more involved in the lives of British people during the Second World War.

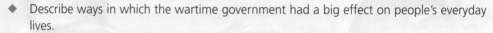

Key Points

You must be able to:

◆ Describe ways in which the wartime government had a big effect on people's everyday lives.

◆ Explain how evacuation, rationing and bombing made the people of Britain more aware of poverty and other social problems such as bad housing.

◆ Explain why the Beveridge Report became so important to people hoping for a better future after the war.

Government intervention during World War Two

In 1939, Britain went to war with Germany. During the war, the government organised the rationing of food, clothing and fuel and gave extra milk and meals for expectant mothers and children. The government also organised the evacuation of children from areas that were likely to be bombed.

The war had a big effect on the public's attitude towards the role of the government in their lives. The British population hoped that after the war their living and working conditions would be better than they had been before the war. A popular saying at the time was 'Post-war must be better than pre-war'.

The Beveridge Report

Mid way through the war, a report written by Sir William Beveridge about social insurance became a best seller! The Beveridge Report identified five giant social problems affecting Britain. By the end of the war, the public hoped a new government would tackle the problems identified by Beveridge.

The next part of the syllabus is about what the Labour Government did to improve the lives of the people in Britain between 1945 and 1951.

Key Points

You must be able to:

◆ Describe what Labour did to tackle each of the five giant problems identified by Beveridge.

◆ Decide how successful Labour was in dealing with those problems between 1945 and 1951.

◆ Explain what is meant by a welfare state that looks after people 'from the cradle to the grave'.

The 'five giants'

The 'five giants' identified by the Beveridge Report were want, disease, idleness, ignorance and squalor.

In other words, the problems were poverty, illness, unemployment, bad education and bad housing.

Between 1945 and 1951, the Labour Government passed a series of new laws that aimed at defeating each of the five giants.

Want was attacked by new laws such as an improved National Insurance scheme, National Assistance for those not in work and child allowance to help ease childhood poverty.

A new National Health Service was started to provide medical treatment for all.

A massive council house building programme was aimed at fighting squalor.

A new education system was started and the school leaving age was raised to 15.

The government also aimed for full employment to give everyone a job and remove the problem of unemployment.

The welfare state

By 1951, it was possible to say that a welfare state had been created. That meant that the government (or state) looked after the welfare (or well-being) of the people of Britain from birth to death, or in other words 'from the cradle to the grave'.

Now practise your skills

The next two questions are examples of the types of questions you can expect in this section.

You will find model answers in Chapter 14.

The answers provided have two purposes.

◆ First, they show examples of good answers to the question.

◆ Second, they provide more information on the topic.

Questions

LO2

Source A: from a recent textbook.

> The Liberal Reforms eased the problem of poverty for the young, sick, unemployed and old. The reforms also attempted to improve the treatment of workers with the introduction of working hours and minimum wages in some industries.
>
> Perhaps the most important long-term change was the change in attitudes towards the 'deserving poor'.

Question: Why were the Liberal Reforms considered important? (Use **Source A** and recall.) (5 marks)

LO3

Source B: from a speech by the Health Minister in 1946.

> This Bill will give us a free universal health service with no insurance qualifications of any sort. We do not intend to limit the amount of help given. There will be a service of local GPs, specialists, hospitals, eye treatment, dental treatment and hearing facilities.

Source C: from a book by a modern historian.

> The service that emerged was paid for very largely by taxes. There was a flood of people seeking treatment. Prescriptions cost twice the figure they had before. Dentists had expected about four million patients a year but twice that number sought treatment. The National Health Service became too expensive and by 1951 it had to introduce charges.

Question: Compare the views of **Sources B** and **C** on the National Health Service. (4 marks)

Chapter 9

SCOTTISH AND BRITISH, CONTEXT 7(B): CAMPAIGNING FOR CHANGE: SOCIAL CHANGE IN SCOTLAND, 1900s–1979

The first part of the syllabus is about the changing role of women in the twentieth century.

Key Points

You must be able to:

- Explain why women wanted the right to vote.
- Describe how the role of women was changing by 1900.
- Describe how women campaigned for the right to vote.
- Describe the reactions of the public and the government to the campaign methods.
- Describe work done by women during the First and Second World Wars.
- Explain why the right to vote was given to some women in 1918 and more in 1928.
- Decide how much women's lives at work and at home had changed by 1945.

Why did women want the right to vote?

Women wanted the right to vote as a way to force greater change in society. They argued that parliament would never listen to their needs for greater reform in the home and at work until they had a way of making the government take notice of them – in other words they wanted the right to vote. The campaign for votes for women is a clear example of people campaigning for change. Pressure groups put pressure on the government to change the law about who could and could not vote.

The role of women around 1900

Many people still believe that women in the later nineteenth century were 'second class citizens' who were inferior to men and unable to vote properly but you should be careful when making statements like that. The idea of women with few rights might have been true around 1850 but was not true by 1900. The Married Women's Property Acts (1870 and 1882) had given women full legal control of all property they had owned when they were married or earned since they married. Education of women had also improved with primary education for girls as well as boys from the 1870s and women being accepted in many universities. Although women still had to leave many jobs when they married, there were many more jobs open to single women by 1900. However, in almost all jobs women worked longer hours and were paid less money than men.

The campaign for change

The National Union of Women's Suffrage Societies (NUWSS) (formed in 1897) believed in moderate, 'peaceful' tactics to win the vote. The NUWSS used a campaign of meetings, pamphlets, petitions and demonstrations. Later the NUWSS was nicknamed the Suffragists in contrast to the later Suffragettes.

You should be careful not to dismiss the campaign of the NUWSS as useless because this was not the case. Membership grew to 53,000 in 1914. Many women joined because they did not want to be linked with the more violent Suffragettes.

The WSPU – the Suffragettes

The Women's Social and Political Union (WSPU) began in 1903 and was led by Emmeline Pankhurst and her daughters. It soon gained the nickname 'the Suffragettes'. At first they held large peaceful demonstrations but from 1910 onwards they became more militant and started to use more violent protest methods. These militant methods included a window smashing campaign aimed at government buildings and acid being poured into post boxes. Other Suffragette targets included the houses of members of the government, cricket pavilions, racecourse stands and golf clubhouses.

When Suffragettes were arrested the government hoped that would be the end of their protests. Instead, women used starvation as a political weapon by going on hunger strike. The government began to force feed the prisoners but the methods used were frequently described as torture and serious health complications often arose as a result of force feeding.

You should understand why the government introduced the Prisoner's Temporary Discharge for Ill Health Act (the Cat and Mouse Act) (1913) and what it was meant to achieve.

You should also be able to give reasons why the Suffragettes were important but perhaps not as important as some people think. Support in parliament for votes for women fell as a result of the militant campaign and the government refused to give in to pressure from violent groups. However, the Liberal Government might not even have discussed votes for women before World War One were it not for the publicity created by the Suffragettes.

How important was the First World War to votes for women?

When Britain declared war on Germany in August 1914 both the NUWSS and the WSPU suspended their campaigns for the vote and did their bit for the war effort. Women performed numerous 'men's jobs' during the war such as conductors on trams and buses, farm workers and, in particular, as munitions workers.

Why did some women gain the vote in 1918?

The 1918 Representation of the People Act gave the right to vote to women over the age of 30 who met certain requirements. The women who had worked long hours and risked their lives in munitions factories were mostly single, in their late teens or early 20s and were not given the vote in 1918.

Undoubtedly the sight of women 'doing their bit' for the war effort gained respect and balanced the negative publicity of the earlier Suffragette campaign.

If you are answering a question on this you must be prepared to balance your answer by considering other reasons for giving some women the right to vote.

By giving the vote to women over 30 the government made sure that there would be no more Suffragette protests after the war. Ten years later (in 1928) there was almost no opposition to giving the vote to all women over 21 on the same terms as men.

How had things changed for women by 1945?

When men returned from the war they wanted their old jobs back and by 1938 the most common job for women was as a domestic servant. But campaigning for change went on. The National Union of Societies for Equal Citizenship was established and campaigned for equal pay, fairer divorce laws and an end to discrimination against women in the professions.

For some women life got easier with labour-saving machines making housework easier, though washing machines and vacuum cleaners were too expensive for most people. For most women work and home life change very little in the 1920s and 1930s.

During the Second World War (1939–1945) women once again 'did their bit'. Many joined the armed forces or again did work usually done by men in factories but when the war ended they went back to being housewives or working for lower wages than men. Real change had to wait until the 1960s.

The next part of the syllabus is about changing patterns of employment in Scotland up to 1979.

Key Points

You must be able to:

◆ Describe Scotland's heavy industries.

◆ Explain why these industries faced problems before and after the First World War.

◆ Describe the protests on Red Clydeside.

◆ Explain why the government was afraid of Red Clydeside.

Scotland at the start of the twentieth century

In 1900 the Central Belt of Scotland was a powerhouse for the production of coal, iron and steel, and for shipbuilding and engineering. Unemployment was low. Many of Scotland's industrial workers earned reasonably good wages and Scottish products were sold around the world. Unfortunately this prosperity did not last.

There were signs that all was not well even before the First World War. In some 'heavy industries' (the name for industries such as engineering, making iron and steel, coal mining and shipbuilding) the world was buying less from Scotland. That meant profits were going down so the owners of the industries tried to keep their profits up by cutting wages and making the workers work harder. As a result the workers who faced wage cuts and long hours joined together in trade unions and went on strike.

You should be able to describe some examples of bad 'industrial relations' before the First World War.

Why did Scotland face difficulties?

One reason for the difficulties was foreign competition. Another reason was that Scotland's finite raw materials, such as iron stone, used for making iron and steel, was running out. Some Scottish factory owners even started building factories abroad to take advantage of lower wage costs. That made more competition for Scotland – but kept the private profits of the owners high. Meanwhile many Scottish owners did not want to spend their profits on new technology and this meant Scotland faced even more competition.

However, the main reason for the difficulties was that Scotland relied far too heavily on old fashioned 'heavy industries'. For example, Scotland employed thousands of workers mining coal but new industries such as oil, gas production and electricity would soon cut demand for coal in people's homes. To put it simply, Scotland did not keep up with the times.

The First World War

The war hid some of the problems in Scottish industry. The wartime demand for iron, steel, coal and ships gave the impression that all was going well for Scottish industry. This was not true. After the war Britain was poorer and weaker than it had been in 1914.

The decline in British exports hit the old traditional industries in Scotland. The drop in Britain's share of world trade meant that less ships were needed for trading which meant less iron and steel was needed. This in turn cut demand for coal. The result was that unemployment became a large problem in the 1920s and 1930s.

Red Clydeside

Red Clydeside was the name given to industrial areas in and around Glasgow where the government feared revolution might break out. The government thought strikes and protests were signs that communists or socialists (Reds) wanted to start a revolution. Most people just wanted better housing and working conditions on Clydeside.

Landlords had increased the rents for poor quality housing and the women of Govan started to protest against such 'profiteering' while their men were away fighting. The government took action towards the end of 1915 by limiting rents to their pre-war level. In this case the rent strikes were a successful campaign against unfair changes.

Tanks were sent to Glasgow to crush any revolution attempt

After the war ended several trade union leaders still campaigned for change. They wanted a 40 hour working week and better working conditions. In January 1919 a huge rally in George Square, Glasgow, frightened the government. Scottish soldiers based near Glasgow were locked in their barracks in case they mutinied and English soldiers and tanks were sent to Glasgow to crush any revolution attempt.

Was there a risk of revolution?

The short answer is no. Many of the protests on Red Clydeside had been about the way the war was being run but not against the war itself. By the end of the war most Glasgow families had lost loved ones in the war. They would not have supported campaigners who suggested the sacrifice of their family and friends had been pointless.

James Maxton, Willie Gallacher and Neil Maclean were key figures during the period. They had strong socialist and communist ideas and although they were in a minority you should be aware of their ideas.

This is the second part of the syllabus about changing patterns of employment.

Key Points

You must be able to:

◆ Explain why the 1920s and 1930s were times of high unemployment in Scotland.

◆ Describe how UK governments tried to help Scottish industries.

◆ Explain why the Second World War delayed the decline of Scotland's older industries.

◆ Describe the effect of conscription on Scottish workers.

◆ Explain why Scottish industry faced more problems after the Second World War.

◆ Explain why North Sea oil and gas were described as a huge bonus for Scotland.

High unemployment

During the 1920s and 1930s Scottish industry was in a slump: businesses shut down, trade collapsed and unemployment increased.

You should be able to explain why there was a slump, especially in the old traditional heavy industries of central Scotland.

In the 1930s the problems got worse when the Wall Street Crash in the USA put the rest of the world into an economic depression. Almost one in every three Scottish workers was unemployed. Many Scots called the 1930s the 'hungry '30s'.

Government intervention

The government tried to help by identifying Special Areas. Depressed areas such as Clydebank got government help to encourage economic development. One of the most famous examples of government help to a traditional industry in a depressed area was the building of the Queen Mary to help shipbuilding on the River Clyde. Towards the end of the

1930s war became likely. Britain began to rearm and and that led to more jobs in the old heavy industries.

The Second World War

The Second World War created jobs. The old industries were busier than ever making weapons and ammunition. Conscription meant that all men from their late teens to their 30s had to be part of the war effort, either in the armed services or in essential war work. With so many young men in the armed forces there were jobs for everyone and women once again moved into jobs that had usually been thought of as 'men's work'.

After the Second World War

In the 1950s the old traditional industries started to face the same problems they had faced after the First World War, especially foreign competition. In the 1960s the government tried to start up new industries such as car production, electronics and chemicals. As the old industries died Scotland looked to the service sector (insurance, banking, retail) for employment but in the 1970s a new unexpected bonus arrived – North Sea Oil.

Oil and the future

In 1967 oil and gas were discovered below the North Sea. Within 10 years over 60,000 people were employed in the industries. Aberdeen and the north-east became a boom area and in Shetland many new jobs were created. Throughout the 1970s, 1980s and 1990s Scotland and the UK benefited from the oil income and natural gas from the North Sea. However, by the 2000s the oil and gas had started to run out and once again Scotland's economy and its workforce faced an uncertain future.

The next part of the syllabus is about education in Scotland between the 1920s and the 1940s.

Key Points

You must be able to:

- Describe what it was like to be at school in the 1920s and 1930s.
- Explain why many children left school with only a basic education.
- Describe the new plans to improve education after the Second World War.
- Explain why some people argued against the new changes to education in the 1940s.

Education up to 1939

After 1872 all children in Scotland aged between 5 and 13 received an elementary (very like primary) education. In 1901 the school leaving age was raised to 14 but by 1914 only 4% of Scotland's children completed their full education. Only 2% of Scottish children went on to university.

By 1939 not much had changed. Many children received no education past primary stage and poorer parents could not afford the fees that some secondary schools charged.

Why did many children leave school with only a basic education?

In most schools most children were taught in large classes and discipline was strict. Teachers were allowed to hit children across their outstretched hands with a thick leather belt. The vast majority of Scotland's children were expected to leave school at fourteen with only basic understanding of the 3 Rs – reading, writing and arithmetic. Most families of working class children also expected their children to go into 'working class jobs' where educational qualifications did not matter.

Some historians argue that Scottish schools did try to educate all their children but other historians think schools were really only interested in producing a small group of well educated children who would fill up 'office jobs' or join the professions. Historian Tom Devine wrote, 'the vast majority of working-class girls and boys left school as soon as they could to enter the factory, pit, farm, office or domestic service.' He explained that most children left school because they were needed to earn a wage. Life was even harder for girls as many families believed girls should not be well educated because they would only get married and have children.

The Education Act (1945)

After the Second World War the government was determined to provide opportunities for all children, especially the poor.

The Education Act of 1945 raised the school leaving age to 15 and provided free secondary education for all children. All children sat an exam at 11 (called the 11+ exam, or the 'Qualy' in Scotland). The results of the exam decided which type of secondary school a child went to. For those who passed the 11+ exam or 'Qualy' the system worked well. They went to senior secondary schools and were expected to stay on at school after 15, go to university or get jobs in management and the professions. However, those children who failed the exam went to a junior secondary, were expected to leave school at 15 and go into unskilled jobs.

Even in the 1940s there was concern about deciding a child's future at 11 or 12 years of age and labelling them as a 'success' or a 'failure'.

The final part of the syllabus is about changes in leisure and entertainment up to 1939.

Key Points

You must be able to:

◆ Describe how entertainment and leisure activities changed in Scotland.

◆ Suggest some reasons why radio and cinema became very popular in the 1920s and 1930s.

Changing entertainment and leisure activities

Between the 1880s and 1939 Scotland's population had more money to spend and more leisure time. Many Scots worked 'only' 48 hours with a half day holiday on Saturday. By 1914, 'trades fortnight' gave some industrial workers 14 days' holiday. In 1938 all workers were given one week's holiday with pay – by law. By the 1930s cars, radios, and cinema were changing how Scots spent their leisure time.

In the theatres and music halls Harry Lauder made gentle fun of old fashioned versions of Scottish identity. In the cinemas, Scots were exposed to the values and fashions of the Hollywood studio dream factories. In dance halls Scots danced to the latest American jazz and big band music.

The Church was an important centre for leisure activities. Children went to youth clubs and Sunday Schools. Churches organised picnic outings to the seaside or countryside, dances and sports days. The Boys Brigade was hugely popular with teenage boys and had over 35,000 members in 1939.

Radio
Radio was a new and hugely popular new way of spending leisuure time. For the first time the outside world was brought into Scottish homes. The only radio station for most people was the BBC which broadcast news, soap serials, drama plays and comedies. The BBC believed its main purpose was to educate rather than entertain but many young Scots thought the BBC was boring and by the 1950s tuned into Radio Luxembourg – the ONLY commercial station that could be heard in Scotland in the evenings.

Fitba' crazy
In the 1930s football was THE spectator sport in Scotland. Within cities, electric trams carried huge numbers of spectators to and from the football grounds while the spreading network of railway lines allowed national leagues to be created and allowed fans to travel between cities in the space of a Saturday afternoon and evening. In 1937 a crowd of 149,515 watched Scotland play England – a world record at the time.

Holiday time
The development of leisure at this time is closely linked to developments in transport. Railways took city people into the countryside and the development of a steamboat and paddle steamers, especially on the Clyde, allowed the urban population in the West of Scotland to go 'doon the watter'. By the end of the 1930s a week's holiday with pay had become the norm and during the summer trades week or fair holiday trains could take holiday-makers further, even to Blackpool or Scarborough.

Dancing
Dancing was another form of mass entertainment that became popular in the 1920s and 1930s. The Saturday night dance became the high point of the week for thousands of young Scots from all social backgrounds. In 1900 the most common place for meeting future husbands or wives had been the church but by 1939 dance halls had become the place for meeting future partners.

Cinema

In the 1920s and 1930s cinemas opened up all across Scotland. As a result 'live' entertainment in variety theatres and music halls became much less popular. By 1935 Edinburgh had over 50 separate cinema buildings and Glasgow had double that number. Even small towns had a cinema. Cinemas provided escapist entertainment and even in the 1920s film stars were influencing the fashions of Scottish youth. For most Scots the cinemas brought the world into their local area for the first time.

The effect on Scottish identity

In the 1880s most rural Scots had strong local accents. There was no opportunity to hear any voice or sound from outside their own area unless they met a visitor or travelled themselves. In the 1920s and 1930s the BBC broadcast radio programmes directly into people's homes and new ideas, fashions and 'proper English' made Harry Lauder's version of 'Scottishness' seem old fashioned.

Now practise your skills

The next four questions are examples of the types of questions you can expect in this section.

You will find model answers in Chapter 14.

The answers provided have two purposes.

◆ First, they show examples of good answers to the question.

◆ Second, they provide more information on the topic.

Questions

LO1

Question: Describe the development of the cinema in Scotland between 1900 and 1939. (5 marks)

LO2

Source A: describes unemployment in the 1930s.

> A whole generation of Scots suffered enormously as a result of the problems of the 1930s. The suffering was not confined to the unskilled ranks of the working class. Where towns depended on a single industry and that industry was hit, it was not unusual to see two thirds out of work. Traditional heavy industries suffered particularly badly.

Question: Why did many Scots suffer badly in the 1930s? (Use **Source A** and recall.) (4 marks)

Questions continued ➢

HOW TO PASS INTERMEDIATE 2 HISTORY

Questions *continued*

LO2

Source B: describes unrest on Clydeside in 1919.

> In January 1919 the Clyde Workers' Committee called a general strike for a shorter working week to avert post-war unemployment. In a subsequent riot, police charged a large demonstration of strikers in George Square, Glasgow. This was enough to persuade the government that it was dealing with a communist rising.

Question: Why did the government fear a communist revolution on Clydeside in January 1919? (Use **Source B** and recall.) (5 marks)

LO3

Source C: is a Suffragette poster from the early twentieth century.

Question: How useful is the source as evidence of problems faced by women in the early 1900s? (4 marks)

Chapter 10

EUROPEAN AND WORLD, CONTEXT 9: IRON AND BLOOD? BISMARCK AND THE CREATION OF THE GERMAN EMPIRE, 1815–1871

The first part of the syllabus is about Germany around 1815.

Key Points

You must be able to:

◆ Describe how the German states were divided before 1815.

◆ Explain why some Germans started to feel a common identity by 1815.

◆ Explain why Metternich was so much against the new ideas of liberalism and nationalism.

◆ Describe what Metternich did to try to stop the spread of new ideas.

Germany before 1815

In 1800, the country now called Germany was split into more than 200 separate states.

Between 1800 and 1815, the German states had been conquered by the French leader Napoleon Bonaparte. Napoleon merged the hundreds of German states into 38 larger states called the Confederation of the Rhine.

Napoleon was not trying to create a united Germany. Instead, he was more concerned with protection against his enemies. Napoleon believed the weak and divided German states were no protection against enemies. Napoleon wanted the River Rhine to be a strong border against France's enemies.

Historians believe that by occupying many of the German states, the French became a common enemy that united German states in a common feeling of dislike of the French.

The German Confederation

When Napoleon was defeated in 1815, the Confederation of the Rhine was changed to the German Confederation. The Assembly of the German Confederation was called the Diet and was definitely not a parliament representing ordinary people.

The new ideas of liberalism and nationalism

The largest power in the German Confederation was Austria but new ideas from Liberals and Nationalists threatened the unity of the Austrian Empire.

Nationalists wanted the states of Germany to join together and rule themselves as one country without any interference from other countries such as Austria.

Liberals were mostly educated, middle class people who wanted a parliament and the right to vote for the leaders they wanted.

Prince Metternich, who was the Austrian Chancellor, was determined that the new German Confederation would stop liberalism and nationalism.

Metternich also became worried about the growth of student societies, many of which supported liberalism and nationalism. The Carlsbad Decrees of 1819 tried to stop the spread of new ideas.

In 1820, the power of the Diet was increased so that soldiers could be used to stop the spread of new ideas in any of the German states.

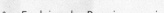

The next part of the syllabus is about the growing power of Prussia.

Key Points

You must be able to:

◆ Explain why Prussia grew in power after 1815.

◆ Describe how the Zollverein made Prussia more powerful.

◆ Explain why Austria did not like the growing power of Prussia.

The growth of Prussia

Metternich believed it was in Austria's interests to keep Germany divided and, therefore, easier to control. However, the German state of Prussia was given more land in the centre and west of Germany as a reward for fighting Napoleon. This new land had big resources of coal and iron, the vital ingredients for an industrial revolution.

As Prussia became richer, other smaller states realised they could make money by trading more freely but trade between the states was difficult.

The Zollverein

In 1818, Prussia started a new customs union that made trade between the different parts of Prussia easier. By the 1830s, the customs union was called the Zollverein.

Business boomed, trade increased and Prussia became rich and powerful. Other German states saw Prussia's success and wanted to join in. By 1836, the Zollverein included 25 German states with a population of 26 million people. The Zollverein showed what could be done if German states co-operated. New ideas began to spread along the new roads and railways between states. The Zollverein helped nationalism to spread and it also helped Prussia's power to increase.

The Zollverein was very important because it was a major reason why Prussia became the most powerful German state.

What did the growth of Prussia mean for Austria?

Prussia became a challenger to Austria for influence over the German states.

It was a prototype or early example of what would happen later – a 'united Germany' under Prussian control which excluded Austria.

Historian William Carr has called the Zollverein, 'the mighty lever of German unification'.

The Treaty of Vienna in 1815 sowed the seeds of future conflict between Austria and Prussia. Prussia became the biggest 'German' state and in hindsight it is possible to see the beginning of the rivalry between Austria and Prussia that would not be ended until Prussia defeated Austria in the war of 1866.

The next part of the syllabus is about the 1848 Revolutions in Germany.

Key Points

You must be able to:

- Describe what Nationalists and Liberals wanted to achieve in the revolutions of 1848.
- Explain why the revolutions failed.
- Describe how Austria seemed to be back in control of the German states by 1850.

The revolutions of 1848

The revolutions of 1848 were important because they were the first attempt by Nationalists and Liberals to challenge Austria's power in Germany.

Liberals and Nationalists wanted a new national parliament in Frankfurt. By the summer of 1848, it seemed as if the revolutions had succeeded. All over Germany the old rulers had given in. The German Confederation had crumbled.

Liberal demonstrators wanted freedom of speech, freedom of the press and political rights.

Nationalist demonstrators wanted the creation of a united country ruled by an elected national parliament.

In May 1848, the Prussian King agreed that a new German parliament called a National Assembly would meet in the city of Frankfurt in May, 1848. He also declared 'Today I take over the leadership of Germany. Today Prussia becomes the leader of a united Germany'.

By the summer of 1848, it seemed as if the revolutions had succeeded.

By 1850, it all seemed so different. The National Parliament in Frankfurt had collapsed, Germany was not united and Austria was back in control.

Why did the revolutions fail?

You must be able to explain why the revolutions of 1848 failed.

Your explanations should be based around the following main points:

1. Arguments broke out within the Frankfurt Parliament. The different social classes could not unite when Austria and the rulers of the German states fought back.

    Another argument was over the future shape of Germany. Should a united Germany be Grossdeutsch (including Austria) or Kleindeutsch (excluding Austria)?

2 The second reason for the failure of the 1848 revolution was the recovery of Austria and its allies in the German states. By 1849, the Austrian army was ready to crush opposition. The Frankfurt Parliament was not strong enough to resist Austria.

3 The third reason for the failure of the revolution was the lack of strong leadership. In the spring of 1848, King Frederick William IV of Prussia said he would lead a united Germany. However, in March 1849 he refused the Crown of Germany.

How did Austria try to regain control?

Austria was determined to destroy the revolutions and the new Chancellor of Austria, called Schwarzenberg, said, 'We shall not let ourselves be thrown out of Germany'. He also said, 'Let Prussia be humiliated and destroyed'.

Austria made clear it was back in charge at a meeting at Olmutz in 1850 where Austria made Prussia promise not to threaten Austrian power again. However, the powerful Prussian economy and the Zollverein were still growing.

The next part of the syllabus is about Bismarck and the unification of Germany.

Key Points

You must be able to:

◆ Describe the three wars Bismarck used to unite Germany.

◆ Explain the different viewpoints about the importance of Bismarck to German unification.

How did Bismarck try to unite Germany?

Before Bismarck began his campaign to unite Germany, he had to make sure of his authority (on behalf of the King) over the Prussian government and its army. First of all, he forced army reforms through the Prussian parliament (landtag).

Bismarck then started to use situations to provoke other countries into conflict with Prussia.

In less than 10 years Bismarck took Germany into three wars.

In 1864, Denmark was defeated after a short war. In 1866, Austria was defeated in only 7 weeks and in 1871 France was defeated by Prussia. The result of the wars was an increase in the power of Prussia and the unification of Germany in 1871.

Ever since, historians have argued over how important Bismarck was to the process of unification.

How important was Bismarck to German unification?

There are three main opinions:

1 Bismarck's importance is that he operated like an architect who had a master plan that he followed in order to build a united Germany. For example, he had to build up the Prussian army, rehearse it against Denmark then defeat Austria before he could tackle France.

2 Bismarck acted as a catalyst, speeding up change that would have happened anyway. Changes such as the Zollverein, the spread of railways and growing Nationalism would have united Germany eventually.

3 Bismarck had the political skill to take advantage of circumstances as they arose and over which he often had no direct control. Supporters of this view believe Bismarck was an opportunist taking advantage of situations as they arose. For example, Bismarck did not cause the Danish demands on Schleswig Holstein or the crisis over the Spanish throne. But he used them both to his advantage.

In January 1871, at the Palace of Versailles just outside Paris, the German princes proclaimed King William of Prussia as the new German Emperor or Kaiser.

Is this the man who united Germany?

There is a view that the process of German unification should really be seen as the story of Prussia's growing power but the fact is that a new country called Germany existed from 1871.

Now practise your skills

The next two questions are examples of the types of questions you can expect in this section.

You will find model answers in Chapter 14.

The answers provided have two purposes.

◆ First, they show examples of good answers to the question.

◆ Second, they provide more information on the topic.

Questions

LO3

Source A: from a speech made by a student at Leipzig in 1820.

> We are an enthusiastic people who are willing to fight for such laws and for liberty and so the Fatherland cannot be conquered. We are all Germans together made equal through speech and customs, all citizens of Germany. A unified people is irresistible.

Question: How useful is **Source A** as evidence about nationalist feeling in the German states after 1815? (4 marks)

Questions continued ➢

Questions *continued*

?

LO2

Source B: from a speech made by Bismarck to the Prussian parliament in September 1862.

Germany does not look to Prussian liberalism, but to its power. Bavaria, Wurttemberg, Baden can indulge in liberalism, but no-one will expect them to undertake Prussia's role. It is not through speeches and majority decisions that the great questions of the day are decided. That was the great mistake of 1849. It is by iron and blood.

Question: Why did Bismarck make this speech to the Prussian parliament? (Use **Source B** and recall.) (5 marks)

Chapter 11

EUROPEAN AND WORLD, CONTEXT 11: FREE AT LAST? RACE RELATIONS IN THE USA, 1918–1968

The first part of the syllabus is about the USA at the end of the First World War.

Key Points

You must be able to:

◆ Explain what is meant by WASP Americans.

◆ Describe the different sorts of people who emigrated to the USA from 1900 onwards.

◆ Explain why people in the USA began to dislike and fear these new immigrants.

◆ Describe what was done to limit the number of immigrants coming into America in the 1920s.

American immigrants in the nineteenth century

Throughout most of the nineteenth century, the USA had an 'open door' policy for immigrants that meant that almost anyone could enter the country. The people who were descended from 'older' immigrants became known as WASPS – White Anglo Saxon (north European) Protestants. Newer immigrants were often Jewish or Catholic from southern or eastern Europe.

Changing attitudes to immigrants in the early twentieth century

In the early twentieth century attitudes towards immigrants began to change fast.

Many Americans feared revolution. In 1917, the Russian Revolution happened. Americans feared Communism might spread to the USA. This fear was called 'the red scare'. In 1919, there was a huge wave of strikes in the USA. Many Americans claimed that the strikes were caused by revolutionary immigrants.

Many Americans feared that more immigrants would make jobs and houses even harder to get. After the Great War, trades union members were trying to get better working conditions but they believed anything done to improve conditions or wages was wrecked by Italian or Polish workers who were prepared to work longer hours for lower wages. Resentment of the new immigrants increased as did the desire to stop them coming into the country.

Immigrants were blamed for the spread of crime.

In the early 1920s, crime was increasing and many American politicians chose to blame immigrants. In 1920, the trial of Nicola Sacco and Bartolomeo Vanzetti for robbery and murder is a good example of how racism and dislike of immigrants linked up with fears of organised crime and political revolution to create a very intolerant attitude towards immigrants during this period.

As a result of increasing worries about the effect of uncontrolled immigration, in the 1920s a series of laws made it harder for immigrants to enter the USA.

You should know what these laws were and how they restricted immigration.

The next part of the syllabus is about how Black Americans were treated in the 1920s and 1930s.

Key Points

You must be able to:

◆ Describe examples of the Jim Crow laws.
◆ Explain how these laws restricted the freedoms and made life difficult for Black Americans.
◆ Describe the activities and beliefs of the KKK.
◆ Explain why the KKK had so much power.

Segregation

Slavery had been abolished in the 1860s but the Southern states of the USA used 'Jim Crow' laws to maintain a segregated society in which white authority was determined to keep control over the Black population. Segregation did not start to break down until 1954.

The right to vote

By 1900, few Black Americans in the South were able to vote easily despite having the legal right to do so. Many Southern states made up rules (called voting qualifications) that made it very difficult for Black Americans to register to vote.

The use of fear

Fear was another way of denying Black Americans their civil rights. Although lynching was illegal the federal government did little to stop it. 'Lynching' meant that a group of people, usually White, would capture, beat and even murder a person they believed was guilty of a crime. In the 1920s and 30s, the Ku Klux Klan (KKK) was involved in terrorising the Black population, especially in the South. Few Klansmen were arrested and in some communities the Klan was helped by local officials.

Many Black Americans had moved north looking for better wages, better jobs and an escape from segregation and fear. However, Black Americans still found themselves segregated into communities and areas of cities that would become known as ghettos.

> ***The next part of the syllabus is about the civil rights protests of the 1950s and early 1960s.***

Key Points

You must be able to:

◆ Explain why there was growing demand for civil rights after 1945.

◆ Describe civil rights protests and demonstrations such as the Montgomery bus boycott, Little Rock High School, Freedom rides, Sit-ins, the March on Washington and King's 'I Have a Dream' speech.

◆ Explain why the civil rights campaigns of the 1950s and early 1960s were successful.

The Civil Rights Movement

Protests and organisations that started before and during the Second World War eventually led to the more organised Civil Rights Movement of the 1950s and 1960s.

During the Second World War, Black Americans started the double V campaign which meant they wanted victory for the USA in the Second World War but also victory for civil rights in the USA. Civil rights means that all people in the country should be treated equally and fairly regardless of colour, religion or gender.

In 1954, the Supreme Court decided that segregation in education was wrong. The Court's decision was a very important victory for the Civil Rights Movement but the problem remained – how to enforce desegregation and put an end to Jim Crow laws.

The decision of the Supreme Court sparked off a new wave of civil rights demonstrations. In 1957, at Little Rock Central High School, Arkansas Black students who tried to join the school were met by racist mobs.

The President of the USA would not accept individual states in the USA ignoring the Supreme Court's decision so he ordered 1000 US soldiers to protect the Black children on their way to school.

Other campaigns of the Civil Rights Movement of the 1950s and early 1960s were aimed at desegregation and changing the Jim Crow laws.

Protests

You should know the detail of the following civil rights protests:

◆ The bus boycott in Montgomery, Alabama

For the first time the Black population showed its economic power. The bus boycott showed what could be achieved by organised, peaceful, non-violent protest.

◆ Sit-ins

Student protests against segregated lunch counters spread across the South. Non-violent protest was met by White racist violence.

By the summer of 1960, there were almost no more segregated lunch counters in the South. National TV coverage and the need to avoid bad publicity had forced restaurants and cafés to desegregate.

◆ Freedom rides

Black and White students tried to use 'Whites only' wash rooms on inter-state highways in the South.

'Freedom' buses were stopped and burned. Passengers were beaten, but the Freedom riders stuck to their non-violent protest beliefs.

The Freedom rides drew national attention, especially from middle-class northerners who were shocked by what they saw on television.

Black students at Little Rock Central High School were greeted with hostility

Martin Luther King

Martin Luther King believed in non-violent, peaceful protest against segregation and discrimination.

He also believed that non-violent civil disobedience was the way to gain civil rights.

The civil rights campaign used the media well. Night after night TV news showed racist Whites beating and attacking peaceful civil rights demonstrators. Public sympathy for the civil rights campaign grew and the US government was forced to take action.

In August 1963, a march on Washington was arranged to increase publicity for the civil rights campaign.

The inspirational speech that Martin Luther King gave to a worldwide TV audience is now called the 'I Have a Dream' speech.

The 'March on Washington' had put the Civil Rights Movement back in the headlines.

The 1964 Civil Rights Act was the most important new civil rights law up to that time and it did a great deal to get rid of discrimination and segregation.

The right to vote

The last big civil rights issue in the South was the right to vote freely. Martin Luther King led a march from Selma to Birmingham, Alabama to publicise the way authorities in the South made it difficult for Black Americans to vote easily.

The marchers were met with police using tear gas and much violence. Television coverage of the march and the attack caused national anger.

In August 1965, Congress passed the Voting Rights Act which removed various barriers to registration.

The Voting Rights Act marked the end of the civil rights campaigns in the South. By 1965, the focus of civil rights protests moved north and the style of protest also changed.

The next part of the syllabus is about the changes in the civil rights protests of the 1960s.

Key Points

You must be able to:

◆ Describe the more militant civil rights protest groups of the 1960s.

◆ Explain why there were disagreements between Martin Luther King and more violent leaders such as Stokely Carmichael.

◆ Explain why Black Americans in the northern cities felt little had been done for them by the early 1960s.

◆ Explain why support for the civil rights campaign decreased by the mid 1960s.

Militant civil rights protests

By the early 1960s, some civil rights campaigners disagreed with Martin Luther King. They did not agree with peaceful non-violence. The most famous of these more militant leaders were Malcolm X and Stokely Carmichael.

You should know the different ideas of Malcolm X and Stokely Carmichael. You should also be aware of more militant groups such as the Black Panthers.

Stokely Carmichael used the phrase 'Black Power' and it became a new slogan and a new idea in the Civil Rights Movement. Black Power included the idea that Black Americans should be prepared to defend themselves and fight back, using violence if necessary.

Black Americans in the north

By 1965, half of all Black Americans lived in the cities of the north and most of them lived in slum areas which were known as ghettos. New laws that ended segregation and made voting easier for Black Americans did little to help the problems of Black Americans in the main cities of the north.

The problems of the urban ghettos marked a major turning point in the campaign for civil rights. Some historians say the city problems were just too big for Martin Luther King. Others argue that Martin Luther King's message of non-violence was old-fashioned and 'Black Power' promised faster results.

Riots

Between 1964 and 1968, many riots broke out during the 'long hot summers' in American cities. In 1968, the assassination of King also added to the impression that non-violent protest was not the way forward. As civil rights protests became more violent, public opinion became less sympathetic to the Civil Rights Movement.

By 1968, civil rights had improved but the issue of Black/White difficulties in America had not gone away.

HOW TO PASS INTERMEDIATE 2 HISTORY

Now practise your skills

The next two questions are examples of the types of questions you can expect in this section.

You will find model answers in Chapter 14.

The answers provided have two purposes.

◆ First, they show examples of good answers to the question.

◆ Second, they provide more information on the topic.

Questions

LO2

Source A: from a letter written in 1916. It describes how the older immigrants felt about the new immigrants.

> It is not surprising that hard working older immigrants are demanding that the USA should no longer be open to just any person from around the world. These new immigrants cannot read or write and many have no money. The truth is that we true Americans want to look after ourselves first of all. We don't want our jobs and homes taken away from us and given to these new immigrants. There are far too many people coming from southern Europe and many of them are Catholic or even Jewish. They are not good Protestants like us.

Question: Why was there tension between the old and new immigrants? (Use **Source A** and recall.) (5 marks)

LO3

Source B: describes the Civil Rights Movement before 1965.

> The late 1950s saw the beginning of a campaign by Black people to improve their position in the USA. Martin Luther King and the Civil Rights Movement led this. They achieved many successes and many people supported them. In 1954 the Supreme Court decided that all schools had to have Black and White students. In 1964 the Civil Rights Act was passed and this stopped discrimination against Blacks. In 1965 a Voting Rights Act was passed and this meant that all Blacks could vote.

Source C: describes the Civil Rights Movement after 1965.

> Some people had become impatient with Martin Luther King's non-violent methods and started to turn to Malcolm X and the Black Panthers. They believed in using violence in order to achieve equality. Many felt that non-violent methods had not succeeded. Indeed many felt that Blacks still suffered from problems. Ghettos (areas of poor housing) were filled with Blacks and many Blacks suffered from poverty. Blacks were faced with inequality every day.

Question: To what extent do **Sources B** and **C** disagree about the success of the Civil Rights Movement in the 1960s? (4 marks)

Chapter 12

EUROPEAN AND WORLD, CONTEXT 12: THE ROAD TO WAR, 1933–1939

 This first part is NOT part of the syllabus but IS important background information which will help you understand what happened between 1933 and 1939.

Key Points

You must be able to:

- Explain what appeasement means.
- Explain why people had lost faith in the League of Nations.
- Explain why Britain adopted the policy of appeasement in the 1930s.

 Background information

Why did appeasement become British policy in the 1930s?

Appeasement grew out of the failure of the League of Nations. The League of Nations was meant to make sure that there would be no repeat of the Great War. The League was intended to ensure world peace through a combination of collective security and disarmament.

In the 1930s, collective security failed because members of the League of Nations were not prepared to get involved in problems that might involve them in a war. Disarmament depended on trust and co-operation but hopes for disarmament had collapsed by 1934.

Britain was concerned about the growing power of Germany. When it was clear the League could not guarantee peace, Britain started to appease Germany.

The policy of appeasement was used by Britain to prevent war.

Appeasement ended when Britain declared war on Germany on 3 September 1939.

 The first part of the syllabus is about the ideas of Nazism and especially Hitler's foreign policy.

Key Points

You must be able to:

- Explain what is meant by foreign policy.
- Explain the connection between the Treaty of Versailles and Hitler's foreign policy.
- Explain the meanings of the words Lebensraum, Aryan and Master Race.

Hitler's foreign policy after the Treaty of Versailles

The Treaty of Versailles was meant to make sure that Germany would never again threaten the peace of Europe. Instead, most Germans were furious with the Treaty. The Treaty of Versailles left Germany bitter and wanting revenge. Hitler and his Nazis rose to power promising to destroy the treaty.

Hitler had four main aims:

1   The Treaty of Versailles had to be destroyed. Most of what Hitler did in the 1930s can be directly linked to Hitler's aim of destroying the Treaty of Versailles.

2   Hitler wanted all German-speaking people to live in one enlarged Germany. That would mean making Germany bigger by taking over other countries such as Austria and parts of Czechoslovakia and Poland.

3   Hitler believed Aryans – or 'pure' Germans – were the master race. Hitler believed the master race had a right to control other 'inferior' people.

4   Hitler claimed that Germany had to have all the land and resources it needed to survive and grow strong, even if it meant taking these things from other countries. This policy aim was called Lebensraum. Hitler's main target for Lebensraum was Russia.

This next part of the syllabus is about how Hitler rearmed Germany and remilitarised the Rhineland.

Key Points

You must be able to:

◆   Describe how Hitler rearmed Germany.

◆   Explain why Hitler remilitarised the Rhineland.

◆   Explain why Europe was concerned by Hitler's actions in 1935 and 1936.

◆   Explain why Britain and France did nothing to stop the remilitarisation.

German rearmament

In 1935, Hitler decided to rearm Germany. Rearmament meant that Germany increased the size of its army, navy and airforce. Between 1933 and 1939, Germany became a much stronger country.

The Treaty of Versailles had demilitarised the Rhineland, which is a large area of the western side of Germany. That meant no German soldiers were allowed in or near the Rhineland but on 7 March 1936 Hitler sent German soldiers into the Rhineland, breaking the Treaty of Versailles.

The next part of the syllabus is about how Hitler took over Austria.

Key Points

You must be able to:

◆ Explain why Hitler wanted to take over Austria.

◆ Explain how Anschluss would help Hitler's ambition to gain Lebensraum.

Anchluss

Anschluss means the joining together of Austria and Germany. Hitler had already tried to take over Austria in 1934 but he had been blocked by Mussolini, the Italian leader. However, by 1938 Hitler and Mussolini were friends and Austria was vulnerable to pressure from Germany.

In February 1938, Hitler was aiming to take over Austria. Schuschnigg, the Austrian Chancellor, suspected that Austria could expect no help from Britain and France.

Schuschnigg planned a plebiscite (also called a referendum) to ask the Austrian people if they wanted to be German or if they wanted to stay Austrian. The plebiscite was planned for 13 March but Hitler ordered Schuschnigg to call it off.

Meanwhile Chamberlain, the British Prime Minister, had said that Austria could expect no help from Britain.

Faced by the reality that he could expect no help from Britain or France, Schuschnigg resigned. On 12 March 1938, German troops marched unopposed into Austria, against the rules of the Treaty of Versailles. That event was called the Anschluss. Britain and France appeased Hitler and did nothing to help Austria.

This part of the syllabus is about the crisis over Czechoslovakia and the Munich agreement.

Key Points

You must be able to:

◆ Describe how Czechoslovakia was vulnerable by 1938.

◆ Explain why Hitler wanted the Sudetenland.

◆ Describe the main stages of the Czech crisis.

◆ Explain why there were such divided opinions about the Munich agreement.

Czechoslovakia and Sudetenland

After Anschluss, Czechoslovakia was in a very vulnerable position. Hitler controlled territory to the north, the west and the south of Czechoslovakia.

Czechoslovakia was a new country created after the Great War. It contained three million German speakers who lived in an area called the Sudetenland. The Sudetenland was the border area of Czechoslovakia

Chamberlain met with Hitler three times to discuss the Sudetenland crisis

near to Germany. It was heavily defended. If Hitler got control of the Sudetenland, it would be easy to make further advances into Czechoslovakia.

In 1938, Europe was close to war because of a crisis over the Sudetenland.

The Munich Agreement

In the late summer of 1938, Hitler began to stir up trouble in the Sudetenland. The British Prime Minister, Neville Chamberlain, was determined to avoid a war. During September 1938, he flew three times to meet Hitler.

The third and final meeting was held at Munich. It was agreed that Germany was to get the Sudetenland almost immediately. Czechoslovakia's leaders were not invited to the Conference and their territory was given away without their agreement.

The Munich Agreement has been a cause of arguments ever since.

Chamberlain claimed to have won 'peace in our time'. Many British people felt that war had been avoided and that Czechoslovakia was not our problem.

On the other hand, some people such as Winston Churchill believed the Munich Agreement was disgraceful. He called the Munich Agreement 'a defeat' and that Britain had 'eaten dirt'.

This part of the syllabus is about the Polish crisis and the declaration of war.

Key Points

You must be able to:

◆ Explain why Hitler wanted to attack Poland.

◆ Describe the effect of the Nazi/Soviet agreement.

◆ Explain why Hitler was surprised when Britain declared war on Germany.

Why did Hitler want to attack Poland?

In March 1939, Hitler tore up the promises made at Munich and invaded the western part of Czechoslovakia called Bohemia and Moravia. Hitler's next move was to create a crisis over Poland.

Poland was created at the end of the Great War, partly from land taken from Germany and Russia. The Polish Corridor was a part of Poland that contained mostly German-speaking people. Hitler complained about the treatment of Germans in the Polish Corridor.

The Nazi/Soviet Non-Aggression Pact

Britain hoped that an alliance with Russia would make Hitler stop because an attack on Poland would risk a war with Russia. But Stalin, the leader of Russia, knew that Russia was not ready to fight.

On 23 August 1939, an agreement was signed between Germany and Russia. It was called the Nazi/Soviet Non-Aggression Pact. The agreement stated that Germany and Russia would not fight each other. The result of the agreement was that Germany was free to attack Poland as Russia would not fight to protect it.

When Hitler invaded Poland he believed he would have a short, easy war.

Hitler was surprised when Britain declared war on Germany on 3 September 1939.

The final part of the syllabus is about why Britain followed the policy of appeasement.

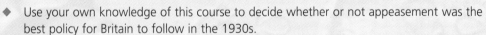

Key Points

You must be able to:

◆ Describe some of the reasons why Britain adopted the policy of appeasement.

◆ Use your own knowledge of this course to decide whether or not appeasement was the best policy for Britain to follow in the 1930s.

Why did Britain adopt the policy at appeasement?

One view of appeasement is that it was a policy of cowardice but recent research has shown there were many reasons why the British government adopted a policy of appeasement. Some of these are outlined below.

1   The British public wanted peace. They feared a repeat of the last war and they feared a new war involving gas bombing of cities.

2   By the mid 1930s, public and politicians alike believed that the Treaty of Versailles had been too hard on Germany and it should be changed.

3   Most leaders, in their rise to power, make extreme statements to gain publicity. Chamberlain believed that Hitler was really a reasonable man who would choose negotiation rather than conflict.

4   Britain's number one priority was its overseas Empire. Any war in Europe involving Britain would threaten the security of the British Empire.

5 Britain had no allies that would help in a war.

6 The heads of Britain's armed forces warned Chamberlain that Britain was too weak to fight. At the same time, Hitler's propaganda encouraged Britain and France to believe that Nazi forces were stronger than they really were.

Now practise your skills

The next two questions are examples of the types of questions you can expect in this section.

You will find model answers in Chapter 14.

The answers provided have two purposes.

◆   First, they show examples of good answers to the question.

◆   Second, they provide more information on the topic.

Questions

LO2

Source A: from a speech by Adolf Hitler on the day he announced Germany would rearm.

> I say this to the leaders of Europe. Yes, we are breaking the treaty but we will get rid of our weapons immediately if other countries do the same. If we are allowed to defend ourselves then we offer a future of peace where all our differences can be discussed equally without using force. But if you attack us we will resist to the last man!

Question: Why did Hitler want to rearm? (Use **Source A** and recall.) (5 marks)

LO3

Source B: Winston Churchill speaks in the House of Commons in October 1938 about the Munich Agreement.

> We have suffered a total defeat . . . I think you will find that in a short period of time Czechoslovakia will have been completely overtaken by the Nazi regime. We have passed a dangerous point in our history. This is only the beginning.

Question: How useful is **Source B** in explaining how people in Britain felt about the Munich Agreement? (Use **Source B** and recall.) (4 marks)

Chapter 13

EUROPEAN AND WORLD, CONTEXT 13, IN THE SHADOW OF THE BOMB: THE COLD WAR, 1945–85

The first part of the syllabus is about what the Cold War means and how differences in ideologies were an important part of the Cold War.

Key Points

You must be able to:

◆ Explain what the Cold War means.

◆ Explain why conflict between the East and West could have led to world war.

◆ Describe the main differences between the ideology of the USSR and the ideology of the USA.

What was the Cold War?

The Cold War lasted from 1945 until 1985. It is the name given to tension between the USA and its allies and the USSR (Russia) and its allies. The Cold War was a time when war could have broken out between the two sides.

Why is the Cold War still important?

The Cold War could have resulted in the destruction of planet Earth because each side was armed with nuclear weapons – more than enough to destroy every single person on the planet.

Nuclear weapons still exist and tension between superpowers can grow again. The history of the Cold War shows that it is possible to sort out arguments without war when the risks are so high.

Why did each side dislike the other?

Each side in the Cold War had its own system of beliefs or ideas about the best kind of government and how people should lead their lives. These systems of beliefs are called ideologies.

The USA believed in Capitalism.

The USA believed in democracy which meant that people had political choices. They could vote and speak freely for or against their government. The media in the West was free. That meant the opinions on radio and tv programmes were not controlled by the government. The USA call its system democratic, in which people are free to make their own decisions.

The USSR believed in Communism.

In Russia's communist system people had no political choice. There was only one political party and anyone who wanted to change the system or spoke out against the communist government was punished. Communists wanted to treat everyone equally but it meant there was a huge amount of government control in people's lives. The media was also controlled by the government.

A communist system is often called a totalitarian system. The government has total control over people. They argue such control is to help the population and protect it from wicked influences – such as democracy!

Each side in the Cold War thought their ideas were best and wanted to spread them around the world.

The differences between the West (the USA and its allies) and the East (the USSR and its allies) caused tension to increase. Each side felt threatened by the other. At several times between 1945 and 1985 large problems and crises developed which could have led to world war.

This part of the syllabus is about why the Cold War started.

Key Points

You must be able to:

◆ Explain why Europe became divided at the end of the Second World War.
◆ Describe the creation of Nato and the Warsaw Pact.
◆ Explain why each side believed military alliances were necessary.

After the Second World War

In the Second World War the USA, USSR and Britain, along with many other countries, had fought against Nazi Germany.

In 1945 Nazi Germany collapsed. At that time the Russians controlled most of eastern Europe while the USA and Britain had soldiers controlling most of western Europe.

Neither side wanted to leave their part of Europe because they thought the other side would take over.

The Americans feared that Russia wanted to make all of Europe Communist. The Russians feared that the West wanted to destroy Russia. The scene was set for tension and conflict.

The USSR was very suspicious of America because the USA had developed an atomic bomb – the first nuclear weapon. That gave the Americans a huge advantage over the USSR. However, by 1949 the Russians had developed their own A-bomb. Throughout the Cold War both sides raced to build bigger and more destructive nuclear weapons. Each side distrusted and feared the other.

Nato and the Warsaw Pact

By the end of the 1940s Europe was divided into a free and democratic western Europe and communist eastern Europe, which was controlled by the USSR. Winston Churchill described Europe as being divided by an Iron Curtain.

In 1949 the USA and its allies made a formal alliance called NATO – the North Atlantic Treaty Organisation. NATO claimed it was a defensive alliance. Countries would fight only if they were attacked by the USSR or its allies.

However, the Russians wanted to protect themselves from attack so they created an alliance with lots of east European countries. These countries were like a huge shield through which the West would have to attack if they wanted to get to Russia. The Russian alliance was called the Warsaw Pact. The allies of the USSR were called Satellite States because they were like satellites in space orbiting round the most powerful member, the USSR.

 ## The next part of the syllabus is about the crisis in Berlin in the early 1960s.

Key Points

You must be able to:

◆ Explain why Berlin became a major source of tension in the Cold War.
◆ Describe the events now called the Berlin Airlift.
◆ Explain why the Berlin Wall was built.
◆ Explain how a crisis in Berlin could have started a world war.

Why was Berlin an area of Cold War tension?

Berlin had been the capital of Nazi Germany and in 1945 it was occupied by the victorious allied armies. When the Second World War ended Germany was divided into zones of occupation and so was Berlin. The Russians, Americans, British and French all controlled a zone each. The problem was that the city of Berlin was in the middle of the Russian zone of Germany.

The Berlin Airlift

The Russians did not like the fact that the Western allies had access into and across Russian controlled territory to get to their zone in Berlin.

In 1948 the Russians stopped all access to Berlin across 'Russian' territory, hoping that the only option for the Western powers would be to abandon West Berlin. Instead the Americans and British flew in supplies to their zones and for many months the West supplied West Berlin by air. All the city's needs were flown in – food, medicines, raw materials for factories, even coal for Berlin's power stations. This was called the Berlin Airlift.

The West knew the Russians might attack the planes but if they did, war would break out. It was a bluff that worked. Eventually the Russians backed down. In May 1949, the blockade of West Berlin was lifted. The USSR's attempt to force the Western powers to abandon West Berlin had ended in total failure, but the tension remained.

The Berlin Wall

By 1961 the Russians were increasingly worried about Berlin. West Berlin was doing very well. Life was good for West Berliners with plenty of food, good wages and a high standard

The Berlin Wall

of living. In East Berlin it was the opposite. Life was hard, wages were low, food supplies were limited and the secret police made people afraid. It was difficult for East Germans to cross to the west along the frontier because it was heavily protected with barbed wire and armed soldiers. In West Berlin it was different. Every day thousands of people crossed between East and West Berlin to go to work. East Germans could fly out from West Berlin and start a new life. Between 1950 and 1961, over 3 million East Germans did exactly that.

The USSR tried to ignore the fact that people were 'voting with their feet' and claimed that West Berlin was a threat. They said spies operated out of West Berlin (this was true, but there were also spies operating out of East Berlin) and that West Berlin was a threat to Russian safety. Overnight, on 13 August 1961, the Russians closed the border. No-one could cross between East and West Berlin. Soon afterwards, the temporary road and rail blocks were replaced by a high, heavily defended wall – The Berlin Wall. The West claimed it was a sign of how people in 'the east' were imprisoned. The Russians claimed it was a wall for their protection. In the following years people were shot trying to escape from the east to the west.

International reaction
The Berlin Wall was a real sign that the 'Iron Curtain' was going to continue dividing Europe. The Americans were angry and moved tanks to the East/West German border in Berlin but there was nothing they could do. The Wall was built in Russian controlled territory. The West was furious but realistic.

Russia had the problem of stopping thousands of East Germans escaping to the west. They could have invaded West Berlin but that would have started a world war.

In the end, the building of the Berlin Wall meant Russia would not have to attack West Berlin and the USA would not have to retaliate. Peace had been kept but tension remained.

This part of the syllabus is about the Cuban Missile Crisis of 1962 when the world came very close to nuclear war.

Key Points

You must be able to

♦ Explain why Cuba became a major source of tension in the Cold War.

♦ Describe the events now called the Cuban Missile Crisis.

♦ Explain how the Cuban Missile Crisis could have started a world war.

Why did Cuba become a crisis point in the early 1960s?

Cuba is a large island about 90 miles from the coast of Florida, USA. For many years USA businesses had big influence over the government of Cuba but in 1959 a revolution led by Fidel Castro had overthrown the old corrupt government. America did not like this revolution so put pressure on Cuba to change back. Castro's Cuba was saved by the USSR who offered to help Cuba. In exchange the Russians wanted to build missile sites on Cuba from which Russian rockets could threaten American cities. At that time Russia had nuclear weapons but no way of 'delivering' them to hit US targets. The USA was simply too far away. By basing missile sites in Cuba the Russians could hit almost anywhere in the USA.

The USA was frightened and angry. They ignored the Russian complaints that American missiles were based in Turkey – within range of Russian cities.

For some time the USA had been using planes to spy on Cuba and take photographs. On 16 October 1962 one of these planes spotted a missile base under construction. At the same time, the USA discovered that a number of Russian ships were on their way to Cuba with missiles on board.

The crisis

The Cuban Missile Crisis lasted from the 16 to 28 October 1962. It was the closest that the world ever came to nuclear war between the USSR and the USA.

As the Russian ships neared Cuba US President Kennedy had to make a serious decision. He announced on television a blockade of Cuba. He knew that Russian ships were sailing to Cuba carrying missiles. Kennedy said that these ships would be stopped and inspected. If they failed to stop they would be sunk. The Russians said that would be an act of war. As the Russian ships got closer to the blockade the world held its breath.

Kennedy's policy was called brinkmanship: each side would push the other to the brink, or edge, of war to see who would back down first. Like two people in a staring contest, who would blink first?

The Russians blinked first. The ships travelling to Cuba were ordered to turn back. In the weeks and months which followed a deal was done between Russia and the USA. The missile sites in Cuba were removed but, secretly, so were some of the US bases in Turkey.

Both sides realised how close they had come to war. As a result a direct telephone link between American and Russian leaders was created. This 'hotline' would allow personal contact and discussion between the leaders and hopefully prevent another crisis developing.

The Cuban Crisis of 1962 is the closest the world has come to nuclear war – that we know about.

This part of the syllabus is about why the USA got involved in a war in Vietnam and what that had to do with the Cold War.

Key Points

You must be able to:

◆ Explain the Domino Theory.
◆ Explain why Vietnam became a major source of tension in the Cold War.
◆ Explain why the USA lost the Vietnam War.

The Domino Theory

In the 1950s the USA became increasingly concerned about the spread of Communism in South East Asia. China had become a communist county in 1949 and the USA believed China would try to spread communism in Asia. The USA believed if they did not take action then communism would spread from one country to another like a line of dominoes with one domino falling and knocking the next domino over. This became known as the Domino Theory. The Americans believed it was their duty to stop communism spreading so countries under communist threat had to be protected.

The Vietnam War

Vietnam is in South East Asia. The country was divided into the communist North Vietnam, and South Vietnam which was under US influence. By the early 1960s North Vietnam was putting pressure on South Vietnam and their soldiers (called Viet Cong or VC for short) were attacking targets in South Vietnam.

US President Lyndon Johnson believed that the Russians and the Chinese were behind the growing Viet Cong pressure in South Vietnam. He also believed that the United States should help to stop the advance of communism in South East Asia. In 1965 Johnson ordered a large force of US Marines into Vietnam and eventually there were over 500,000 American combat troops fighting in the war.

Huge American resources poured into Vietnam. Bombers tried to destroy VC bases and supply routes into the south but mostly these attacks failed. The VC used the jungles to their advantage and fought a 'low tech' war using donkeys, mules and living in secret tunnel networks, sometimes right beside US bases. American troops were worn down by these guerilla warfare tactics and became trapped in an unwinnable war. As US casualty figures got bigger the US public began to ask 'Why are we there?' and 'Should we be there?'

Why the USA lost the war

By the later 1960s public opinion in America and the West turned against the war. Huge anti-war demonstrations were held and movies and pop songs reflected the anti-war mood of the country. When the US government introduced 'the draft', protests erupted across the country. The draft meant that young American men were forced to join the army – or run away and became criminals for refusing to fight.

When Richard Nixon became the next US president he knew US policy had to change. He began to withdraw troops from Vietnam and in 1973 the last American forces left South Vietnam. It was the first war that America had ever lost and Vietnam became a communist country.

Despite the power of the USA, it had been unable to win the war. By 1968 the American people wanted their troops home. They saw no point in a war which showed their sons being killed 'live' on TV. But the world had changed too. By 1970 the USA had a much better relationship with the communist countries and were now not worried about the Domino Theory. President Nixon had a policy of making friends with the Russians. It was called Détente.

This part of the syllabus is about attempts to reach agreements between the USA and the USSR and the agreements reached to reduce the number of nuclear weapons.

Key Points

You must be able to:

◆ Describe the policy of defence known as 'MAD'.

◆ Explain the meaning of Détente.

◆ Describe agreements about nuclear weapons made between the USSR and the USA, especially the SALT treaties.

Was MAD mad?

Most of the 1960s relations between the USSR and USA were bad. After the Cuban Missile Crisis a telephone hotline had been set up which allowed the leaders of each country to talk directly to each other but there had been little progress in limiting the number of nuclear weapons each side possessed.

In fact each side had so many nuclear weapons that people referred to the policy as MAD. This meant Mutually Assured Destruction. If either side started a nuclear war they would be sure that their country would be wiped out too. It seemed mad, but perhaps it prevented either side thinking they could win a nuclear war. It was, however, a risky policy.

What was Détente?

Détente means reaching agreements to lessen tension. It was a word used to describe the meetings and agreements between the USA and the USSR in the 1970s aimed at reducing the number of nuclear weapons and making the possibility of war less likely.

Why did Détente take root?

By the early 1970s political leaders in the USA and the USSR were more ready to talk to each other about lessening the tension in the Cold War. One way to do that would be to cut the number of nuclear weapons stockpiled by each side.

Each side had their own reasons to accept peaceful discussion rather than increasing tension. The USA leaders knew the public were anti-war after Vietnam and were not likely to support more military spending. President Nixon also needed the help of Russia to reach a peace agreement in Vietnam. Russia was concerned about the expense of the arms race and wanted to reduce the cost.

Discussions about limiting nuclear weapons

One of the main reasons the superpowers were willing to talk about limiting nuclear weapons was fast-changing technology. New and bigger weapons systems were expensive and neither side wanted an escalating arms race costing billions of dollars. But discussions were made more difficult by the different sizes and power of nuclear weapons. Some carried one warhead. Others carried several and each one could be directed at a separate target. Technology was also developing anti-ballistic missile systems (ABMs), whereby attacking nuclear missiles could be intercepted and destroyed before reaching their targets.

The discussions were called Strategic Arms Limitation Talks – or SALT for short.

The first SALT Treaty was signed at a conference held in Moscow, in May 1972. The SALT I treaty restricted the numbers of missiles and missile launchers held by each side.

Seven years later a new treaty – SALT II – was signed between the USA and Russia in June 1979. SALT II was aimed at slowing down the arms race. It was intended to last for 6 years but when the USSR invaded Afghanistan in 1979 the US government refused to sign the agreement.

In the 1980s Détente seemed dead. A new US President, Ronald Reagan, called the USSR an 'Evil Empire' and promised to dump communism into 'the ash can of history'. President Reagan believed that the period of Détente in the 1970s was a mistake. He believed the Russians only understood strength, and he began a programme of expanding and improving America's nuclear weapons. It seemed as if a second Cold War was beginning but by 1990 communism in the USSR was dead.

It seems as if Reagan was right. Quite simply the USSR could not afford to build more and better weapons to keep up with the USA. By 1990 the USSR economy was in ruins and political collapse followed. With the collapse of communism the Cold War ended.

Now practise your skills

The next three questions are examples of the types of questions you can expect in this section.

You will find model answers in Chapter 14.

The answers provided have two purposes.

◆ First, they show examples of good answers to the question.

◆ Second, they provide more information on the topic.

Questions

LO1

Question: Describe the events which led to the formation of the Warsaw Pact in 1955. (5 marks)

LO2

Source A: an extract from Winston Churchill's 'Iron Curtain' speech on 5 March 1946.

> From Stettin on the Baltic to Trieste on the Adriatic, an iron curtain has descended across the continent. Behind that line Communist Parties in all these eastern states have been raised to power. They are all subject to a very high measure of control from Moscow. This is certainly not the liberated Europe we fought to build up. Nor is it one which contains the essentials of permanent peace.

Source B: an extract from a speech made by Stalin, reported in 'Pravda' on 13 March 1946.

> There can be no doubt that Mr Churchill's position is a call for a war on the USSR. The Soviet Union's loss of life has been several times greater than that of Britain and the United States put together. The Soviet Union cannot forget its losses. And it is not surprising that the Soviet Union is anxious for its future safety and is trying to ensure that governments loyal to the Soviet Union should exist in neighbouring countries.

Question: In what ways and for what reasons do **Sources A** and **B** differ in their attitudes towards the division of Europe in 1946? (4 marks)

LO2

Source C: an extract from *The Times* on 15 January 1980 about attempts at disarmament.

> Since arms negotiations are hopelessly bogged down, there seems to be no alternative to the continuing arms race. There is no available means for reviving Superpower détente. Russia has publicly rejected the NATO offer to discuss nuclear weapons which is another sign that the SALT process is failing.

Question: Why did the détente process appear to collapse by 1980? (Use **Source C** and recall.) (5 marks)

Chapter 14

MODEL ANSWERS TO QUESTIONS IN THE CONTEXT UNITS

This section will provide you with model answers to the questions set at the end of the preceding context units as well as advice on how to answer them.

Chapter 6 – Scottish and British, Context 2: Wallace, Bruce and the Wars of Independence, 1286–1328

Questions and Answers

LO1 Question: Describe the methods used by King Edward to take control of Scotland after the defeat of John Balliol. (5 marks)

LO1 Answer

'Edward tried to take control of Scotland by taking away its independence.

First of all he took away Scotland's holiest relics. They were like lucky charms. Scots believed the relics brought Scotland good luck.

All of Scotland's important knights were forced to promise to support the English king.

Edward of England made one of his friends the new ruler of Scotland.

Edward took away the Stone of Destiny. It was important to the Scots. The stone was used in the ceremony that made new kings.

Edward called Scotland his "land". He did not call Scotland a country or a kingdom.

England took over the town of Berwick.

All the Scottish crown jewels were taken away to England.

All Scottish taxes were collected and sent to London.

In conclusion Edward tried to take away Scotland's independence, its freedom and its identity.'

Why is this a good answer?

It has a straightforward introduction, a middle section that gives lots of information and it ends with a clear conclusion which does not just repeat the introduction but adds a couple of new ideas about freedom and identity.

The question asks you to describe what Edward did to Scotland and the answer gives more than five examples so this should easily get full marks.

It also explains some of the things Edward did and does not just make a list of things done to Scotland.

Questions and Answers

LO3 Question: How reliable is **Source A** as evidence of disagreements in Scotland about who should be King of Scots? (4 marks)

LO3 Answer

'This source is valuable as evidence of disagreements about who should be king. After Alexander III died Scotland was divided between supporters of Bruce, Balliol and Margaret until her death in 1290.

The fact that it is written by supporters of Bruce suggests there must be supporters of other people at the time and also disagreements between them.

Bruce had supporters who refer to him as "true heir" and any challenge to Bruce as "unfair".

There is proof of disagreements by referring to "you and your supporters" wanting Balliol to be king. The source then asks for Edward of England to help Bruce become king, which is "his right".

There is clearly an argument going on about who should be king with different groups campaigning on behalf of their leader. All this proves there were disagreements over who should be king.

On the other hand the source does not provide any reasons why there was such disagreement or anything about the strength of the claims. However it does show that there were strong feelings and disagreements at the time.'

Why is this a good answer?

This is a tricky question.

It is not enough to answer about the reliability of the source. You must always check what a source is meant to be reliable for.

In this case, the answer keeps mostly to the point about disagreements and there is not much time wasted proving it is biased. That is not the question! This question starts by placing the source in context briefly, quotes well from the source and links directly and relevantly to the main question about 'disagreements' five times.

Chapter 7 – Scottish and British, Context 6: Immigrants and Exiles: Scotland, 1830s–1930s

Questions and Answers

LO2 Question: Why did many Irish come to Scotland in the nineteenth century? (Use **Source A** and recall.) (5 marks)

LO2 Answer

'There were several reasons why Irish people came to Scotland in the nineteenth century.

Better wages were a big attraction and so was regular employment. Most Irish immigrants had been farm workers who had faced low wages and times of no work at all. In Scotland work was also available for the whole family in the factories of central Scotland. That would mean the family could earn more than they had done in Ireland.

There were also push factors that forced people to emigrate. The potato famine gave people a choice of starve or emigrate. Even before the famine, poverty was a huge problem in Ireland and the prospect of better jobs caused many Irish to think of emigration as an answer to their problems and an opportunity for a better life.'

Why is this a good answer?

The answer contains at least three points from the source and each of these points is explained or developed in a way that helps answer the question.

There are at least two main points of recall and each one of them is explained so there is plenty of opportunity for a marker to award this five marks.

Questions and Answers

LO3 Question: How far do **Sources B** and **C** agree about emigration from Scotland? (5 marks)

LO3 Answer

'The sources agree to a large extent. In sources B and C overpopulation in the Highlands is mentioned as a reason for emigration. The sources also agree that "crop failures" were a cause of migration and source C gives more detail by referring to "distress during the potato famine". The sources also agree that emigration was helped by government organisations such as the Emigration Commission and the Highland and Island Emigration Society.

Both sources mention Canada as a place where Scottish emigrants went to but Australia is only mentioned in source C.

However the sources only refer to emigration from crofting areas in the Highlands and give no information about Lowland migration.

The only point where they do not match is when B refers to "Civilian emigration to Canada was encouraged by the problems caused to the crofter's way of life by improvements on Highland estates" but there is no mention of that reason for emigration in source C.'

Why is this a good answer?

The answer starts with a direct overall answer to the question. It then gives five detailed examples of ways the sources agree or have common points between them. It then goes on to give one example of how the sources do not always agree or match up. There are more than enough comparisons to earn full marks.

Chapter 8 – Scottish and British, Context 7(a): From the Cradle to the Grave? Social Welfare in Britain, 1890s–1951

Questions and Answers

LO2 Question: Why were the Liberal Reforms considered important? (Use **Source A** and recall.) (5 marks)

LO2 Answer

'The Liberal Reforms were considered important because they eased the problem of poverty for the young, sick, unemployed and old. They also improved the treatment of workers with the introduction of working hours and minimum wages in some industries.

Perhaps the most important long-term change was the change in attitudes towards the 'deserving poor' represented by the Liberal Reforms.

The old were helped with an old age pension of 5 shillings (25 pence) a week to people over 70.

Children were helped with free school meals for the poorest children. In 1907 school medical inspections started but it was not until 1912 that free medical treatment was available.

The sick were helped by the National Insurance Scheme of 1911 that helped insured workers.

The unemployed also benefited from the National Insurance Act of 1911. Insured workers got seven shillings (35 pence) a week for a maximum of 15 weeks while out of work.

Labour exchanges were started which were similar to job centres now. Workers could find out easily what jobs were available in their area.

Overall the Liberal Reforms were important because they helped people who were poor through no fault of their own and because they helped lay the foundations for later reforms leading to the Welfare State.'

Why is this a good answer?

The first point to note is that the question asked the student to use the source AND recall.

This answer does that.

The first part of the answer uses the source thoroughly picking out all the relevant points.

The second half of the answer then goes on to include quite a lot of relevant detail explaining how the reforms helped the old, young, sick and unemployed.

Finally, there is a conclusion that answers the main question directly by stating why the writer thought the reforms were important.

Questions and Answers

LO3 Comparison Question: Compare the views of **Sources B** and **C** on the National Health Service. (4 marks)

LO3 Comparison Answer

'Source B is a primary source from a speech about the Health Service that had not yet started. It gives a positive impression of what the health service will provide.

On the other hand source C is a secondary source written with the benefit of hindsight long after the NHS started. It provided a more realistic assessment of what really happened.

The sources disagree about the cost of the new service.

Source B claims that "this Bill will give us a free universal health service" but source C writes that the costs of the service were "paid for very largely by taxes" and that "Prescriptions cost twice the figure they had before". Source C goes on to write that by 1951 some charges had to be introduced to pay for the services.

The sources also disagree about the level of demand for help from the NHS. Source B thought that there would be "no limit to the amount of help given" but source C writes about "a flood of people seeking treatment" so that soon "the National Health Service became too expensive".

The sources do agree that the service was very popular. Source B states that the service will meet the health care needs of the people and C writes about "the flood of people" wanting treatment.

Maybe the main difference between the sources is that B is trying to boost the idea of an NHS before it started while source C is showing what it was really like.'

Why is this a good answer?

This question had a top mark of four.

This question makes five direct comparisons.

It compares points they disagree on but also points that are similar.

The comparisons also consider the origin of the sources and not just their content.

Chapter 9 – Scottish and British, Context 7(b): Campaigning for Change: Social Change in Scotland, 1900s–1979

Questions and Answers

LO1 Question: Describe the development of the cinema in Scotland between 1900 and 1939. (5 marks)

LO1 Answer

'Cinema started in Scotland with small 'one reel' films in small halls or theatres. Movies were silent and accompanied by a piano player. During the First World War the government used cinema to show news and propaganda films such as 'The Battle of the Somme'. Silent film comedies with Charlie Chaplin were popular. In Scotland early films often just showed filmed stage performances by old theatre stars such as Harry Lauder – but they were silent.

By the 1920s Scottish audiences were watching mostly Hollywood films and stars such as Clara Bow and Rudolf Valentino made Scots more aware of fashion.

Films provided escapist entertainment. By the 1930s the 'talkies' and colour films had arrived. Musicals, romantic films and adventure films were popular. Scots tried to look like the celebrity stars such as Errol Flynn and Clark Gable.

By 1939 there were hundreds of cinemas in Scottish cities and towns. Some were dirty and cheap and were known as fleapits. Others were like dream palaces. These were huge buildings that could look like ancient Greek theatres with star shaped lights in the ceilings to make it look like the audience was sitting in the open air. Thousands of people sat together watching the same film.

Big movies such as Snow White and Gone With the Wind were hugely popular. By 1939 many Scots went to the cinema two or three times each week.'

Why is this a good answer?

It is a good answer because it answers the question.

There is a lot of different detailed information that could be used here. For example, you may have studied the cinema in your area of town.

This answer takes a general view of cinema in Scotland. The important things to note are that it covers the time asked about 1900–1939, it deals with the cinema and gives examples of films, cinemas and stars.

This is an entirely recall answer and does describe the cinema in Scotland. It provides more than enough recalled information to justify five marks and shows that the writer has accurate and relevant and detailed knowledge about the cinema in Scotland between 1900 and 1939.

HOW TO PASS INTERMEDIATE 2 HISTORY

Questions and Answers

LO2 Question: Why did many Scots suffer badly in the 1930s? (Use **Source A** and recall.) (4 marks)

LO2 Answer

'Most working Scots in central Scotland depended for work on old traditional industries such as coal mining, iron and steel making, and shipbuilding.

Many Scots suffered badly "as a result of the problems of the 1930s." This refers to the economic depression that swept around the world after the Wall Street Crash in the USA. World trade collapsed and unemployment increased.

Many Scots also suffered because they relied for work on old traditional heavy industries such as coal mining, iron and steel making, and shipbuilding. When these industries "suffered particularly badly" so did the Scots employed in them.

The source also says "Where towns depended on a single industry … it was not unusual to see two thirds out of work." The town of Clydebank depended on shipbuilding and only the building of the Queen Mary helped the town recover.'

Why is this a reasonably good answer?

The answer uses source content and recall.

The source states that Scots suffered in the 1930s and the answer starts by outlining the causes of the problems.

The answer mostly relies on using recall to develop points in the source and about unemployment.

The source did not give a lot of information but since the question is only worth four marks answers can be shorter and enough points are made in this answer to score at least three, if not four, marks out of four.

Questions and Answers

LO2 Question: Why did the government fear a communist revolution on Clydeside in January 1919? (Use **Source B** and recall.) (5 marks)

LO2 Answer

'By January 1919 there were attempts at communist or socialist revolutions taking place across Europe, for example, in Germany.

The government was afraid that workers on Clydeside might be inspired by the revolution that took place in Russia just over a year before. The Russian revolution had started with workers joining together and striking. When the British government heard that the red flag of revolution was flying above a protest demonstration in Glasgow they were afraid a revolution could start there. There were also some socialist leaders involved in the demonstration who wanted a revolution, such as McLean and Maxton.

The government had been worried about protests on Red Clydeside for some time. During the war there were protests about the war. When unemployment rose after the war the government worried that angry workers would join revolutionary groups.'

Why is this a good answer?

The answer uses both the source and recall.

From the source it develops the points about the formation of workers committees and the workers wanting a general strike. It mentions riots and demonstrations.

Recall is used to explain similarities with the start of the Russian Revolution. More recall is used by stating that socialists such as McLean and Maxton were involved. It explains how the red flag flying in Glasgow worried the government.

This answer also makes the point that communist revolutions were being attempted across Europe at this time so it was not unreasonable for the government to be worried.

Questions and Answers

LO3 Question: How useful is the source as evidence of problems faced by women in the early 1900s? (4 marks)

LO3 Answer

'The poster is partly useful as evidence of problems faced by women in the early 1900s.

The poster is primary evidence from the early 1900s produced by the Suffragettes and showing their point of view. It illustrates the point about women lacking freedom by showing a woman trapped within bars. It also suggests that women are treated no better than convicts and lunatics when it comes to having the right to vote in parliamentary elections – none of them have the vote.

The poster also suggests that women are finding it difficult to improve their rights ("where shall I find the key").

On the other hand the poster, produced by the WSPU, does contain some bias showing an educated woman in contrast to convicts and lunatics. The poster does not show many of the problems of working class women such as low wages, long hours and domestic abuse which were some of the reasons the Pankhursts started the WSPU.

Overall the poster draws attention to the lack of the vote by suggesting that some women certainly were qualified to justify getting the vote.'

Why is this a good answer?

The answer is balanced by looking at the usefulness and also the limitations of the source.

Positive evaluation points about the source are made by commenting on the content and provenance of the poster. The answer then considers the bias in the source and also the limits of the poster in answering the question set.

Chapter 10 – Europe and the World, Context 9: Iron and Blood? Bismarck and the Creation of the German Empire, 1815–1871

Questions and Answers

LO3 Question: How useful is **Source A** as evidence about nationalist feeling in the German states after 1815? (4 marks)

LO3 Answer

'The speech is a primary source written a few years after 1815 by a nationalist arguing that "a unified people is irresistible". The source is therefore relevant to the question.

The content of the source shows how nationalists felt at the time and provides information on the reasons why they thought Germany should be united. Germany is referred to as the "Fatherland" and the aim of nationalists was to achieve liberty or freedom for their country. The student also uses some of the nationalist arguments such as all Germans spoke the same language and had similar customs. The student believes "We are all Germans together".

This student might have been taking a risk to publicise his views because after the Carlsbad Decrees student societies were shut down and students spreading nationalist ideas could be punished.

On the other hand student societies were a minority and many Germans did not know about or support nationalist ideas just after 1815.'

Why is this a good answer?

Both the origin and the content are used well. The source is used to provide evidence in the answer and good recall is used. There is also some balance in the answer towards the answer. All of this helps to make the evaluation a good answer.

Questions and Answers

LO2 Question: Why did Bismarck make this speech to the Prussian parliament? (Use **Source B** and recall.) (5 marks)

LO2 Answer

'Bismarck had recently become minister president of Prussia and faced a problem. He had been appointed by the King to push through army reforms that would cost money that would be raised by increasing taxation.

Bismarck claims that Prussia has an important role to play in Germany unlike states such as Bavaria, Wurttemberg and Baden.

***Questions* and *Answers* continued ➤**

Questions and Answers continued

Bismarck argues that it is not enough to discuss and vote on new ideas. He said that was the mistake of 1849 when the Frankfurt parliament had collapsed. Change would only happen by force and Prussia would only be successful if it had a powerful army. Bismarck wanted to persuade parliament that a strong army was necessary.

Bismarck might also have wanted to show himself as a strong minister president as a warning to other countries such as Austria.

Bismarck might also have wanted to encourage Prussian politicians to support his ideas about increasing Prussian power.'

Why is this a good answer?

First of all it is relevant to the question. The whole answer is focused on explaining why Bismarck made the speech to parliament.

Relevant and detailed recall is used to place the speech in context in terms of the situation Bismarck found himself in when he became minister president.

In summary, the answer gives more than enough reasons from recall and the source easily to justify five marks.

Chapter 11 – Europe and the World, Context 11: Free at Last? Race Relations in the USA, 1918–1968

Questions and Answers

LO2 Question: Why was there tension between the old and new immigrants? (Use **Source A** and recall.) (5 marks)

LO2 Answer

'The writer thinks real Americans should be able to look after themselves and he dislikes the new immigrants because they cannot read or write and have little money. The writer also thinks there are too many coming from southern Europe and these new immigrants take away homes and jobs from real Americans.

The writer does not like the large numbers of Catholic or Jewish immigrants because they are different from him. He refers to Protestants like himself as good.

From recall Americans were afraid that immigrants brought crime with them such as Sacco and Vanzetti and even political revolution. "Small town" America thought immigrants brought wicked new ideas with them which would destroy the old American way of life. For all these reasons tension grew between new and old immigrants in America.'

Questions and Answers

LO3 Question: To what extent do **Sources B** and **C** disagree about the success of the Civil Rights Movement in the 1960s? (4 marks)

LO3 Answer

Overall source B gives a positive slant on the Civil Rights Movement. It says "They achieved many successes". On the other hand source C takes an opposite view questioning the success of the non-violent approach.

In detail source B suggests MLK was an important influential person who led the CRM and it claims, "many people supported them". However source C states, "people had become impatient with Martin Luther King's non-violent methods". They started to support more violent organisations such as the Black Panthers. Source B also suggests "many people supported" non-violent protest but source C writes that some people "believed in using violence in order to achieve equality".

The sources also disagree about the effectiveness of the campaigns. B writes the CRM "achieved many successes" but C states people felt "non-violent methods had not succeeded".

Finally B lists some of the successes such as schools being integrated, a Civil Rights Act and the Voting Rights Act. On the other hand C writes that, "Blacks still suffered from problems", "Ghettos (areas of poor housing) were filled with Blacks" and "many Blacks suffered from poverty" and "Blacks were faced with inequality every day". This suggests that C does not think great improvements had been made whereas B thinks the non-violence of Martin Luther King had been very successful.'

Chapter 12 – Europe and the World, Context 12: The Road to War, 1933–1939

Questions and Answers

LO2 Question: Why did Hitler want to rearm? (Use **Source A** and recall.) (5 marks)

LO2 Answer

'According to the source Hitler wanted to rearm for defensive reasons. He claims that Germany might be at risk of being attacked. He states that Germany would get rid of its weapons "if other countries do the same".

Another reason he wanted to rearm is deliberately to break the Treaty of Versailles, which forced Germany to disarm. From recall, one of Hitler's main aims was to destroy the Treaty of Versailles. Another aim was to take over areas of Europe. At first these places had German-speaking people in them but later Hitler wanted to take over Russia to achieve Lebensraum. To do all these things Germany would need to be strong so Hitler rearmed. Finally rearming Germany would create jobs as soldiers or making weapons. Hitler had promised to give all Germans jobs. Rearming would do that.'

Why is this a good answer?

The answer uses a fairly simple but effective method. First of all it deals with information taken from the source. The answer includes a quote plus some information from the source put into the student's own words and then a little bit of explanation.

The student then makes it clear that the next paragraph is from recall and there are at least four different pieces of recall included.

By using this way of answering the question, the student has understood the instruction 'use source and recall' and has used detailed and relevant information to answer the question. The point about being relevant is important because there is a lot of information in the source about offers of peace and what Hitler will do if he is allowed to rearm. However, none of that information is relevant to the question asked about why he did it.

Questions and Answers

LO3 Question: How useful is **Source B** in explaining how people in Britain felt about the Munich Agreement? (4 marks)

LO3 Answer

'The Munich Agreement was signed at the end of September 1938. It seemed to avoid the risk of war over the Czech Crisis. Chamberlain returned from Munich promising "peace in our time" but other people felt that Britain had betrayed Czechoslovakia and had given into Hitler's bully tactics.

Source B is partly useful in showing how British people felt about the Munich Agreement. Churchill was a well-known politician who had growing support in Britain. The source also comes from the time just after the Munich Agreement when feelings were high. Churchill is deliberately attacking the policy of appeasement and trying to encourage more people to speak up against it. However Churchill was only a part of a large minority who felt Britain had been humiliated. People such as cartoonist David Low supported Churchill and thought Munich was a defeat. On the other hand most people in Britain did not agree with Churchill. Newspapers praised Chamberlain as a hero who had saved Britain.

They were only too happy that war had been avoided.

In conclusion the source is partly useful in showing one of the differing opinions about the Munich Agreement.'

Why is this a good answer?

Overall this answer shows off knowledge about the Munich Agreement, the Czech crisis, British attitudes and also answers the question asked!

The first paragraph sets the scene and places the source in context.

The second paragraph deals with the content of the source, shows that the writer understands the source and makes a decision about how useful the source is. The writer then gives a balanced answer weighing up the importance of Churchill and his opinion compared with other views at the time.

The answer then finishes with a short conclusion directly answering the question.

Chapter 13 – European and World, Context 13: In the Shadow of the Bomb: The Cold War, 1945–85

Questions and Answers

LO1 Question: Describe the events which led to the formation of the Warsaw Pact in 1955 (5 marks).

LO1 Answer

'The reason given by the USSR for the creation of The Warsaw Pact was the decision to allow West Germany to join NATO.

The real reason has its roots in the causes of the Cold War. The USSR was very afraid of attack from the West and tension had been increasing between the East and the West since 1945.

The USSR claimed to feel threatened by NATO and needed to defend themselves.

The West believed that the Warsaw Pact allowed the USSR to base its troops in member states and keep closer control over its satellites because the USSR and its allies combined their armed forces under one command – in reality the USSR.

On the other hand the Russians were worried that West Germany was being allowed to rearm and that a strong West Germany would be a threat to peace in Europe.

The Russians were also worried that Nato was encouraging countries in the Near and Middle East to form military alliances to plan attacks on the USSR and its allies.

In conclusion the Warsaw Pact was formed because the West had create an alliance system called Nato in 1949. It had developed bigger and better nuclear weapons and the Russians felt threatened.'

Why is this a good answer?

In an LO1 question like this it is important to have a brief introduction and conclusion and a development section providing about five pieces of recall. This answer does those things with seven different points of recall, although the theme that Russia felt threatened is repeated.

Questions and Answers

LO2 Question: In what ways and for what reasons do **Sources A** and **B** differ in their attitudes towards the division of Europe in 1946? (4 marks)

LO2 Answer

'Both sources refer to the division of Europe by an "Iron curtain" after the Second World War.

The USSR took control of eastern Europe while the West was made up of democratic, independent countries.

Questions* and *Answers continued ➤

Questions and Answers continued

Source A is by Churchill who had been British Prime Minister. He was against Communism and believed the USSR was using its power to dominate eastern Europe. He said, "Communist Parties in all these eastern states have been raised to power. They are all subject to a very high measure of control from Moscow."

On the other hand Stalin, leader of the USSR, believed Churchill wanted war against the USSR and that Britain and the USA was a threat to the USSR. He said, "Churchill's position is a call for a war on the USSR."

Churchill described Europe as divided by an Iron Curtain and claimed the USSR was a threat to peace. He described eastern Europe as "not the liberated Europe we fought to build up. Nor is it one which contains the essentials of permanent peace".

Stalin takes the opposite view. He claims that the USSR needs to defend itself and states "the Soviet Union is anxious for its future safety".

Both sources show the tension and suspicion that existed at the end of the Second World War. The West, led by the USA, feared the USSR wanted to spread communism over all of Europe while Stalin believed the West wanted to destroy communism. Neither side would trust the other so Europe became divided between two different ideologies.'

Why is this a good answer?

The question asks two things – to compare the sources and also explain why the two sources have such different opinions.

The answer briefly sets the answer in context then makes clear comparisons between the sources using extracts from the sources that are well explained. The answer then explains why the Cold War developed after 1945 and therefore explains the different opinions in the sources.

Questions and Answers

LO2 Question: Why did the détente process appear to collapse by 1980? (Use **Source C** and recall.) (5 marks)

LO2 Answer

'Détente was the meetings and agreements between the USA and the USSR in the 1970s aimed at reducing the number of nuclear weapons. However, *The Times*, on 15 January 1980, reported that "arms negotiations are hopelessly bogged down" so a reason for détente failing was that no agreement could be reached on limiting nuclear weapons. Another reason for détente's failure was that there was "no available means for reviving Superpower détente", meaning that there was no way to force the USA or the USSR to reach agreements. *The Times* also said that "Russia has publicly rejected the NATO offer to discuss nuclear weapons" which looks like the USSR was refusing to cooperate.

When the Russians invaded Afghanistan, the USA refused to keep the agreements it made in SALT II. The USA also had a new President called Reagan who believed the USSR was "an evil empire" and that détente was a sign of weakness. By 1980 the détente process had appeared to collapse because there was a lack of trust between the superpowers.'

Why is this a good answer?

This is a five mark question which asks the candidate to use the source and recall. To be safe it is best to use three points from the source and three from recall.

Here the source extracts are explained only slightly but the answer recovers with four good pieces of relevant recall, one being used to set the answer in context and another being used to provide an overall conclusion to the answer.

Conclusion

Now you are ready for your exam. Good luck.

On the other hand, when a famous golfer was told he had been lucky when he holed a long putt, he replied, 'You know, the more I practise the luckier I get'. In other words, you don't need luck. You have worked hard and you know what to expect in the exam. Eat and sleep well before the exam. Allow plenty of time to arrive at the place you will sit the exam. Avoid arguments before the exam and be as relaxed as you can be.

Use time carefully and all will be well.